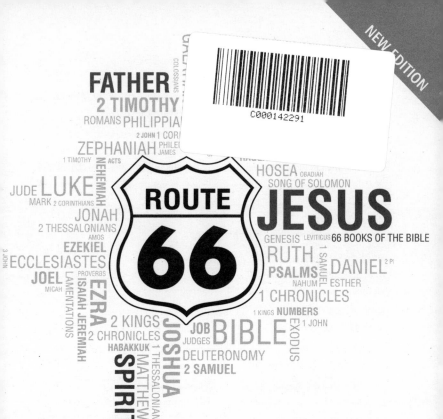

A CRASH COURSE IN NAVIGATING LIFE WITH THE BIBLE

# KRISH KANDIAH

MONARCH
BOOKS

Published by
**Monarch Books**
www.lionhudson.com

Part of the SPCK Group
SPCK, 36 Causton Street, London,
SW1P 4ST

ISBN 978 0 85721 994 7
eISBN 978 1 80030 003 3

First published in the UK in 2011 by Lion Hudson IP and Elevation (a publishing imprint of the Memralife Group)

**British Library Cataloguing Data**
A catalogue record for this book is available from the British Library.

Printed and bound in the UK, May 2021, LH26

# Contents

Preface                                              5
How to use *Route 66*                                8
Introduction: the journey                           10

## 1 Living faithfully (the narrative literature)
The ride of our lives                               22
Mirror, signal, manoeuvre                           25
One eye on the road                                 28
Signposts                                           31
Which way now?                                      35
Small Group Study 1                                 38

## 2 Living distinctively (the law)
White lines                                         42
Right-hand drive                                    46
Map upgrade                                         49
No entry                                            53
Concept cars                                        57
Small Group Study 2                                 60

## 3 Living poetically (the psalms)
Playlist                                            64
Repeat mode                                         67
Soundproof                                          70
Speed-bumps                                         74
Getting closer                                      78
Small Group Study 3                                 82

## 4 Living discerningly (the wisdom literature)
Crossroads                                          86
Speed-traps                                         89
Biting-point                                        93
Turbo-charged                                       95
Connections                                         99
Small Group Study 4                                103

# 5 Living prophetically (the prophets)

Viewpoints 106
The end of the tunnel 111
Recipe for disaster 115
Wrong direction 119
Long way round 123
Small Group Study 5 127

# 6 Living infectiously (the gospels)

Used cars 130
Donkeys and Beatles 135
Soundbites 138
Skyline 142
Conversations 146
Small Group Study 6 150

# 7 Living purposefully (the epistles)

Hyperdrive 152
Off track 157
Go the distance 161
Transmission 165
Pimp my ride 169
Small Group Study 7 173

# 8 Living hopefully (the apocalyptic literature)

Happy ending 176
Predictions 180
Pictures 184
Number plates 187
Write the future? 191
Small Group Study 8 194

The 8-week Bible reading challenge 197
Tools worth investing in 200
Source material 202

# Preface

Christians claim that the Bible is a sacred text, the foundation of our faith, a guidebook for life and a tangible connection to God himself. Our courts still offer witnesses to place a hand on the Bible and swear to tell the truth; the integrity of the justice system stands by it. BBC Radio 4 continues to recognize the Bible as a survival tool should we find ourselves stranded indefinitely on a desert island. And our book industry records the Bible as the best-selling book of the year – every year. Churches preach it, schools teach it, and most of us have it close at hand in the form of an app on our phone. YouVersion claims their Bible app has been installed on 400 million devices worldwide. Access to, and respect for, the Bible is arguably higher than ever.

However, despite this, the Bible remains a closed book, unknown territory and an ancient relic for many of us. It *is* a closed book while it sits on our shelves gathering dust or just takes up valuable memory space on our phones. It *is* unknown territory while its language and its customs make it feel far removed from our everyday realities. It *does* often seem like an ancient relic, best assigned to the past where it knew better days, merely a historical curiosity with little or no useful value to us today.

Yes, the Bible is a closed book. It is always closed in court, always unopened on Desert Island Discs, and too often left closed on my own bedside table and smartphone. But I wonder, could a closed book suggest an invitation?

There is often a tussle in our house about being the first person to open a new book. I love it when I win – the book is pristine, no pages are turned, and the spine is unbroken. I get to be the one who discovers what is going on inside. I get to be the one who shares the revelations and twists and quotes with the family or allude to them on social media. I can blaze the trail to become engrossed by the plot and enriched by the themes. Perhaps our increased unfamiliarity with the Bible is a blessing in disguise – we can read it as though it were the first time, discovering the treasure and wisdom and stories that could change our lives. *Route 66* helps us uncover and discover fresh treasure in the pages of Scripture.

And yes, the Bible is unknown territory. In fact, it is a lot of unknown territories, written over thousands of years and over three continents. There have been countless attempts to translate it into languages that we understand, and writers, theologians, and preachers could spend millennia attempting to explain the various parts of it. But I wonder, could unknown territory suggest an adventure?

Travel companies spend a lot of money advertising far-reached, exotic places around the globe, some barely accessible. Full-page photographs present us with a language, culture and landscape poles apart from our usual everyday life. But somehow, we are intrigued; we are helped to believe that by investing in this experience with our hard-earned finances and our valuable free time, our minds will be broadened, our relationships will be strengthened, and we will find rest and relaxation in the process! Travelling through the Bible could be like visiting this incredible unknown foreign land just waiting to be discovered and experienced – and the more remote it is, the more invigorating it could be. *Route 66* helps us navigate around the exciting undiscovered landscapes of the Bible.

And yes, the Bible is an ancient relic. It was written thousands of years ago to cultures devoid of technology, democracy and civil liberties. It doesn't fit into our political debates, it doesn't adjust well to our consumerism, and it doesn't provide quick-fix lifehacks or a dummy's guide to life in the twenty-first century. It simply doesn't belong in our times. But does this, I wonder, make it even more precious?

As a child, Indiana Jones was one of my heroes. I loved the way he would risk life and limb to sneak past booby-trapped tombs full of bottomless chasms and hidden spears. At the end of his quest was normally an ancient undiscovered relic. Bringing this treasure to the modern world often had more present-day implications than Indiana Jones could predict: for example, discovering the Ark of the Covenant led to a shift in the global power balance. Could the same be true with the

Bible? Even though the Bible is an ancient treasure, it is still packed with power, containing major implications for the whole of humanity.

Our ancestors knew what they were handling. They described the word of God as sharper than any two-edged sword; sharp enough to slice through joints and marrow, and soul and spirit. They knew it to be sweeter than honey, and more precious than gold. Those who discovered its treasures and believed in its future significance, risked their lives to spread its message far and wide, and preserve it for generations. Early converts faced persecution and even hungry lions in a sports arena for it. William Tyndale burned at the stake for daring to translate it into English. Smugglers faced imprisonment if they were caught carrying it. Kings and emperors have risen and fallen because of their stand on the Bible. Wars have been waged, and heroes have been discovered. Just as history has changed because of the Bible, so can the future. *Route 66* helps us not to get trapped into thinking the Bible has no impact and relevance for today's world, but to open our eyes to see the incomparable value of the ancient treasure that is in our hands.

This God-breathed, Spirit-infused, Jesus-honouring book has changed my life – and not just once. It was through reading the Bible for myself that I became a follower of Jesus. The Bible called me to change my career. It was through hearing the Spirit of God through its pages that I was called to found a charity and work globally with governments for child welfare reform. This has taken me all over the world – including on my own Route 66 journey from Chicago to Los Angeles. The unexpected situations I find myself in because of the Bible, also lead me back to the Bible time and again to seek fresh answers, inspiration, motivation, strength, and wisdom.

The invitation to discover a closed book, the opportunity to take time to explore new destinations, and the realization that this ancient relic is as valuable and powerful now as ever, are available to all of us who dare to take a journey through and with the 66 books of the Bible.

# How to use *Route 66*

Welcome to *Route 66*, a journey to discover how the 66 books of the Bible help us to know God and how to live for him. This book is a crash course in enjoying the breadth and depth of the Bible, and is packed full of practical help.

There are three ways you can use this book:

### On your own
If your Bible reading needs some inspiration, then this book provides a user-friendly way to get inspired and skilled up to handle the Bible better. Take your time, aiming to read it over eight weeks. There are forty "travel journal" Bible studies for you to put into practice the lessons you are learning along the way, and also an 8-week Bible-reading challenge for the more adventurous.

### With your small group
An African proverb says, "If you want to travel fast, travel alone, but if you want to travel far, travel together." Reading *Route 66* will be a lot more beneficial if you read it with others. With stand-alone small-group questions at the end of each section, this book makes an ideal 8-week small-group series.

### With your church
The Bible is God's word for all his people, and to have the whole church literally on the same page of the Bible can make for exciting and effective discussions and discipleship. *Route 66* contains a variety of ways this can work:

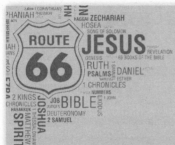

⊕ **8 THEMES:** These are the main segments of the Bible based on genres, which can be used as the basis for an 8-week sermon series.

⊕ **40 TRAVEL-JOURNAL STUDIES:** These are ideal as daily inspirations helping individuals to practise what has been discussed in each chapter.

⊕ **8 SMALL-GROUP STUDIES:** At the end of each week you will find some thought-provoking Bible-study questions for discussion in small groups.

⊕ **8-WEEK BIBLE-READING CHALLENGE:** At the end of the book is a suggested plan for reading through the whole of the Bible in eight weeks.

# Introduction: the journey

*I never travel without my diary. One should always have something sensational to read in the train.*

**Oscar Wilde**[1]

I agree. Train journeys are the ideal place for reading books. Reading redeems the long hours in a waiting-room and generates a force-field of privacy in a crowded carriage. But although Oscar Wilde's diary contained some riveting material, my own diary is probably one of the most drab and dreary books on my shelf. Give me a good novel any day, or anything off the *The Times* bestseller list. A magazine or a newspaper will do otherwise, and failing that, there is always my Bible lurking somewhere at the bottom of my bag. The Bible is often so low down on my list of favourite literary texts, it may as well be propping up my bookshelf along with my Russian-language copy of *War and Peace* and an ancient copy of the *Yellow Pages*.

I am grateful for the occasional long train journey to remind me that reading the Bible can be relaxing, refreshing, even rewarding. But imagine that our time spent in the Bible (reluctantly or readily) could actually change our direction and destination. Imagine that instead of travelling with the book, we start travelling by the book. Here are three illustrations to help us to grasp these distinctions.

## Transportation or transformation?

My train journey to work with my fellow commuters is an inconvenience to be endured. Our heads and hands are buried in our newspapers and our ears are jammed by headphones in an attempt to trick our senses into believing we are anywhere else but on the 7:03 into Marylebone. The second part of my commute used to be on the suffocating, sweaty, stuffy London Underground, but since I bought a bike this part of my journey has become an adventure, although unfortunately no less sweaty! My commute by bike is about transformation as well as transportation. I can now feel calf muscles where there once was only amorphous fat. I now understand the city not as a knotted maze of roads, but more like a familiar friend. As we travel through the Bible

---

1   Wilde O., 1895, *The Importance of Being Earnest*, Act 2.

together, we will see that reading it is not a chore to be endured but an opportunity to be transformed. The aim of *Route 66* is not just to teach us how to navigate our way around the Bible, but how to navigate life with the Bible, allowing God's word to change our faith and our lives and our character en route.

## Information or translation?

Some journeys are about gaining information, like the open-top bus tour of Belfast I went on in the rain to fill a spare hour between meetings. I now know all sorts of information about that beautiful city that may possibly come in handy in a pub quiz but is otherwise surplus to the requirements of daily life. It was a very different city tour to one I had been on several years earlier in Tirana, the capital city of Albania, with a friendly bilingual tour-guide. Not only did I acquire information about the historical landmarks, I discovered where to buy a loaf of bread, how to phone home, and what to say when I needed to access my bank account. This was to be vital knowledge for managing everyday life for the following three years as my wife and I worked there.

As we become more familiar with the contours of the Bible, we are not just collecting lots of theological data about the literary landmarks to store in the recesses of our minds. The aim of *Route 66* is to give us skills to help us to translate the Bible, not literally from Hebrew, Aramaic, or Greek, but practically into the nitty-gritty of everyday life.

## Obligation or invitation?

My journey to visit 3 Wellington Road, where a frail and elderly lady lived, was always a drag. My mum, usually on some mission to bring charity and culinary pleasure, had to physically unplug me from my games console and usher me out of the door. I made those walks a lot of hard work. My feet were moving, but my head was down and my heart was far, far away; physically I was present, but I was emotionally absent.

My first visit to 10 Downing Street was not like that. My heart was beating fast and there was a spring in my step as I happily abandoned everything and anything else I was doing that afternoon. Our journey with the Bible is less about obligation and more about invitation. The aim of *Route 66* is to break away from seeing the Bible as a book we are obliged to study, and to see it more as an invitation into the company of the King of kings.

I aced my driving theory test. By memorizing the Highway Code, I could tell you the precise stopping distance of a car travelling at 60 mph in the wet and I could identify any traffic sign that you could throw at me, whether low bridges, duck crossings, or biohazards. I walked out of that office with my head and my certificate held high and then begrudgingly got into the passenger seat of the car. Despite passing the theory exam, I was still totally incapable of getting a car to go from A to B. Three months later, I succeeded in providing my driving-test examiner with several near-death experiences in a 25-minute test of faith. I am not sure whether it was the stray piece of scaffolding in a skip which barely missed his head as I took a corner, or the whiplash he got from my emergency stop, or simply the look of sheer panic on the faces of passers-by that led him to fail me.

There is a huge difference between theory and practice, not only regarding learning to drive, but also when reading the Bible. Knowing the theory of how to navigate the Bible is a very different set of skills to knowing how to navigate life with the Bible.

Unfortunately for many of us, theoretical knowledge is all we have. Like a geography lecturer at a university who can describe the way that the glaciers, rock formations and wind-speed patterns affect the north face of Everest, but who is totally incapable of making an assault on the mountain, we are often full of information that does not translate into action.

But theoretical knowledge is important. The basic information I learned in my driving theory test is invaluable to me every time I drive a car. In the same way, it is vital to grasp some theoretical knowledge if we are going to allow our life journeys to be shaped by the Bible. *Route 66* contains plenty of theory, gathered together from the best Bible scholars around, but let's not be satisfied with that – *Route 66* also aims to inspire us to take it to the next level.

When we learn to drive, there is no substitute for simply getting behind the wheel, crunching the gears into place, feeling, hearing, or even smelling the biting-point of a clutch, and sensing the responsibility of steering a potential killing machine through crowded town streets. Handling the Bible is no different. The good book is not going to do us any good unless we are willing to move from theory to practice. Whether we are reading the Bible by ourselves for the first time, or passing on a Bible truth to somebody else for the umpteenth time, it is as the rubber hits the road that we experience the fact that the Bible is far more than just a book.

When I finally passed my driving test, I got into the car, taking full responsibility for my life and the lives of hundreds of other road-users and future passengers. I said goodbye to my instructor, never seeing or hearing from him again. I was officially a safe driver, but the question remained then as now – how will I drive today? Theoretical knowledge and good habits together are not quite sufficient. We need to get our attitude in gear too.

Richard Briggs, in his book *Reading the Bible Wisely*, poses this riddle: *Who are you?*

> *You believe that*
> *… the Scriptures are the word of God*
> *… they apply to all of life*
> *… it is important to interpret them properly*
> *… God still speaks through his Scriptures today*
> *… God's word is for everyone, even those who do not realize it.*[2]

In Jesus' day the Pharisees would have affirmed all of these statements. As religious leaders they had the same view of the Bible as many of us, a sound doctrine of Scripture, excellent background information and rigorous habits for Bible reading and memorization. Yet when the Bible's promised Messiah, Jesus Christ himself, stood physically in front of them, they failed to recognize him. I would like to suggest a four-point check of virtues that we should monitor, pursue and develop[3] to help us beware of the blindness of the Pharisees.

## Open to listen?

Google Maps has transformed my confidence, efficiency and stress levels while driving. However, I always turn the volume off. I don't mind being shown the right way to go, but being given verbal instructions by the SatNav lady makes me feel like a naughty or stupid schoolboy! And when I get told off for pulling into the services for fuel, or making

2   Briggs, R. S., 2003, *Reading the Bible Wisely*, SPCK. Used by permission of Wipf and Stock Publishers, www.wipfandstock.com
3   Kevin Vanhoozer lists honesty, openness, attention and obedience as the interpretive virtues that are needed to respect the givenness of the text of Scripture. See Vanhoozer, K. J., 1998, *Is There a Meaning in This Text? The Bible, the reader and the morality of literary knowledge*, IVP, p. 377, and also Briggs, R. S., 2010, *The Virtuous Reader: Old Testament Narrative and Interpretive Virtue*, SPCK.

a detour to pick up some cash, I could easily strangle that annoying voice that barks over and over, "Turn around where possible." I wonder if we have the same attitude to the Bible. We may be happy to turn to the Bible when we feel lost or when we want comfort or reassurance, but we resist the voice of the Holy Spirit, particularly when we think we know better or don't want to change course. Jesus rebuked the Pharisees for their obstinate refusal to listen and saved the heartbeat of his teaching for those who had ears to hear.[4]

## Open to learn?

The Pharisees often approached Jesus with a question. But mostly it was not because they were looking to catch something of Jesus' wisdom or passion, but because they were trying to catch Jesus out. The Pharisees came so preloaded with theological convictions that when God's Son spoke to them, there was no room in their minds or hearts for what he had to say. Sometimes we need to be prepared not only to listen, but also to learn and relearn. I have had to do this with mathematics recently. I am more than happy to listen to my son talk about his maths homework, but in order to understand and help him, I need to relearn the subject the way he has learned it. It is so totally different from the way I was taught that I may as well learn to write with my left hand while I am at it! The humility I need to allow my eight-year-old to teach me a whole new world of "chunking" and "sharing" is nothing compared to the humility we need to accept that God's word gives us a whole upside-down view of how we should live our lives.

## Open to change?

Imagine driving along the inside lane of the motorway, gradually gaining on a slow caravan in front. You check your mirrors, and spot a thirty-ton shiny red truck hurtling down the middle lane. Nobody in their right mind would promptly forget that thirty-ton shiny red truck and pull out anyway. The whole point of spotting the oncoming hazard is to take appropriate action. James applies this mirror principle to reading the Bible, challenging us to be committed not just to observing the information, but to applying and obeying the instruction.[5] Jesus

---

4   Jesus uses this phrase often, normally connected with a parable. Mark 4:9, 23. "The efficacy of Jesus' proclamation of the kingdom depends on faithful hearing." Ryken, L., Wilhoit, J. C., Longman, T., Duriez, C., Penney, D. & Reid, D. G., 2000, *Dictionary of Biblical Imagery* (electronic ed.), InterVarsity Press, p. 224.

5   James 1:21–23.

told countless parables to show the Pharisees the error of their ways, but their refusal to change led them so far away from God that they executed his Son. The only person who really equips us to hear and apply the word of God is the Spirit of God. As David Jackman puts it: "There is a special appropriateness in this, for it is the Holy Spirit who inspired the Word and it is still his great tool in the work of bringing people to Christ and building them up in the faith."[6] It is only as we allow the Holy Spirit to do his work that we will be open to the word of God to change us.

## Open to critique?

Jesus says things to the Pharisees I would love to say to some Christians I know! He calls them whitewashed tombs, a brood of vipers, hypocrites and more. But my temptation betrays just how like the Pharisees I am, falling into the same trap of being willing to criticize others and unwilling to consider my own flaws and failings. Jesus puts it much more creatively: "You strain out a gnat but swallow a camel."[7] Or elsewhere: "Why do you look at the speck of sawdust in your brother's eye and pay no attention to the plank in your own eye?"[8] We cannot fault-find or name and shame others in our churches, because Jesus tells us that we need to be willing to apply the Bible's teaching to ourselves first. Rather than using the Bible as a weapon to attack others, do we have the softness of heart that allows God to lovingly expose our own shortcomings?

Recently I drove my car over my laptop. Not deliberately, I hasten to add. I sadly mistook my suitcase for a snowdrift and reversed over it. Now there are certain advantages in flattening things – it makes packing a lot easier as less space is taken up, it is kinder on the environment as less energy is used, and it reminds us of the temporary nature of material possessions. But flattening can also mean that the purpose, functionality and sheer beauty of things get utterly and fatally destroyed.

Often, to make the Bible easier to grasp, we flatten it. Some sermons are like spiritual steamrollers ignoring the nuance, substance or background of the text, and forcing it into a twenty-minute, three-point, monotonous, bullet-point structure. Unfortunately it is not only preachers who handle the Bible this way. When we read the Bible for ourselves,

---

6   Jackman, D., 2006, *Spirit of Truth: Unlocking the Bible's Teaching on the Holy Spirit*, Proclamation Trust Media, p. 9.
7   Matthew 23:24–26.
8   Matthew 7:3.

we can easily approach the different books with the same expectations. This is the reason why many of us attempt to read the Bible through from cover to cover and give up when we move from the storytelling style of Genesis and Exodus to the lists in Leviticus. This is why many of us stick to the familiarity of the gospels and epistles and don't venture much into the foreign territory of the rest of the Bible. But flattening the Bible like this leaves us feeling flat too, which can be fatal for our spiritual lives.

A great deal of our Christian literature is an attempt to flatten the Bible into another type of book.

But God did not send us a spiritual repair manual, full of step-by-step practical advice for maintaining and repairing our spiritual lives.

God did not send us a bumper sticker with pithy quotations to help us smile or regain perspective.

God did not send us a full service history with exact specifications of how previous owners had lived up to the responsibility of being a Christian.

God did not send us the Highway Code with all theological terms defined and rules for salvation clearly stated to keep us on the right side of the law.

God did not send us an MOT certificate declaring who was roadworthy of heaven.

The Bible is not a theological textbook, a small book of calm, a list of rules and regulations, a get-out-of-hell-free card or a fast-paced page-turner ideally adaptable for the big screen. The Bible is God's voice in our hands – he chose to speak to us in a book that is diverse in style, broad in context, grounded in history, deep in theology, true to life and perfect for growing faith whoever and wherever we are.

The variety of the Bible mirrors the variety and breadth of human experience – our personalities, our moods, our decisions, our learning preferences, our life experiences, our flaws, our gifts, our struggles, our needs. If we could learn how to better appreciate the diversity, details and depths of the Bible, we would be better equipped to navigate through the complexities of the journey of faith in today's world.

God, in his wisdom, knew that we needed every word of every page of every book of the Bible, and God knew we needed the variety of styles (which we will call genres) that we are going to look at more closely in the rest of this book:

1. Narrative
2. Law
3. Psalms
4. Wisdom
5. Prophetic
6. Gospels
7. Epistles
8. Apocalyptic

## Genres as terrains

Scholars sometimes devote lifetimes of study and endless books to just one verse, chapter or letter of the Bible, so attempting to open up the whole of the Bible in just eight sections may seem daunting. In order to cover the key bases, we are not going to provide in-depth study of each book of the Bible, or get into the fine details of the historical, theological and cultural controversies. Rather, *Route 66* aims to be a "crash course" in driving through the different terrains of Scripture, that will launch you into discovering more of the Bible for yourself.

The historic US highway Route 66 is unique because of its variety of terrain. From cosmopolitan cities to mysterious ghost-towns, from colourful, scenic mountains to sandy, flat plains and deserts, it is precisely the variety of the landscape that attracts people to drive its length for sheer pleasure as well as out of necessity.

Scripture is similarly diverse, from the panoramic pronunciation of the origins of the universe to the painstaking details of the template for the Temple; from the comic relief of the pantomime that is the book of Esther to the agonizing emotional rollercoaster of Psalms; from Jeremiah's desert experience to Jesus' despair in the garden of Gethsemane to John's vision of the celestial city.

This book cannot possibly be an exhaustive list either of biblical or individual terrains.[9] Even the most meticulous driving preparation classes do not cover every possible driving scenario. Rather, the instructors train learner drivers to handle a number of different types

---

9   For more detailed analysis see Greidanus, S., 1988, *The Modern Preacher and the Ancient Text: interpreting and preaching Biblical literature*, Eerdmans; Fee, G. D. & Stuart, D., 2003, *How to Read the Bible for all its Worth*, Zondervan; Duvall, J. S. & Hays, J. D., 2005, *Grasping God's Word*, Zondervan; Osborne, G. R., 1991, *The Hermeneutical Spiral: A comprehensive introduction to Biblical interpretation*, IVP.

of driving conditions so that they build up a skill set that they can then apply in the wide spectrum of real-world driving situations.

When Chesley Sullenberger was forced to crash-land a jet plane carrying 155 passengers into the Hudson River in February 2009, he managed to do so safely not because he had been trained for that precise eventuality, but because he was able to extrapolate common sense from his thorough training in all sorts of standard and emergency conditions.[10] As we engage with the different genres to develop Bible-reading and life-navigating skills, we should see this as a starting point that can then be useful in all sorts of other contexts.

### Genres as gears

Secondly, in everyday life we are often subconsciously aware of different genres of writing, and we instinctively adapt our reading style. We do not attempt to read the telephone directory from cover to cover, or sing the contents of a Chinese takeaway menu, or memorize the small print of an insurance certificate. Learning to discover the right reading style for each genre can be likened to finding the right gear for the terrain we are crossing. Fifth gear may be better than first gear on a motorway, but a low gear is far more useful on a hazardous route. So for some parts of Scripture we may feel like we are cruising, while in others it is more of an uphill struggle, a stop–start city route, or a slow crawl. Nevertheless, every gear or genre is given to us to be useful at some point.

### Genres as perspectives

Finally, although the gears are vital, it would be a scary experience to travel with someone who drives with their eyes glued to the gear-stick. An experienced driver will not even look down but instinctively change to the right gear while focusing on where they are going. It would be a similarly fatal mistake to focus so much on the genres that we miss the whole point of Scripture – which is to draw us into a transforming relationship with the living God. To keep their eyes on where they are going, drivers have a variety of perspectives – the windscreen, side windows, rear-view mirror, dashboard display, map screen – all of which are used in different and complementary ways to enable them to drive wisely. In the same way, the Scriptures provide us with windows on God's character, and a variety of different perspectives that help us not

---

10  Wright, N. T., 2010, *Virtue Reborn*, SPCK, p. 7.

only build a composite picture of who God is, but also a composite way of thinking and travelling through life with God.

Looking back, I cannot tell you exactly what I did on any one of my driving lessons. I do remember having to recover my magnetic L plates off the side of a busy country road, and I will never forget that dreaded five-way roundabout I could never join, much to the annoyance of the growing queue of irate drivers behind me. But even though I don't remember how I learned to master three-point turns, hill starts or busy roundabouts, I do know that before my lessons I was not able to drive, and now I can. I know that once I struggled and sweated at each manoeuvre and junction, but now general road-sense is second nature. As we travel through this book, many of the tips and habits may feel clumsy at first, but as we persevere and practise and progress, we will develop good instincts for navigating life with the Bible.

The Bible is more than just a book. It is more than just a library. It is more than the number-one bestseller of all time. It is more than a priceless ancient literary artefact. It is more than a useful guide to life. It is more than a precious collection of love-letters. It is more than a treasure-trove of truth. God created the whole vast universe with just a dozen words, and then put 800,000 more words into our hands.

Each word was chosen for a reason. This is why reading the Bible and navigating life have to go hand in hand. As we look more closely at the beauty of the poetry, the precision of the laws, the passion of the prophets and much more, it is my prayer that our all-powerful God would reveal himself to us and work powerfully in us, so that we can live to please him in every way.

> *But as for you, continue in what you have learned and have become convinced of, because you know those from whom you learned it, and how from infancy you have known the holy Scriptures, which are able to make you wise for salvation through faith in Christ Jesus. All Scripture is God-breathed and is useful for teaching, rebuking, correcting and training in righteousness, so that the man of God may be thoroughly equipped for every good work.*[11]

---

11    2 Timothy 3:14–17.

# 1

# Week 1: **Living faithfully**

*The narrative literature and its application to life*

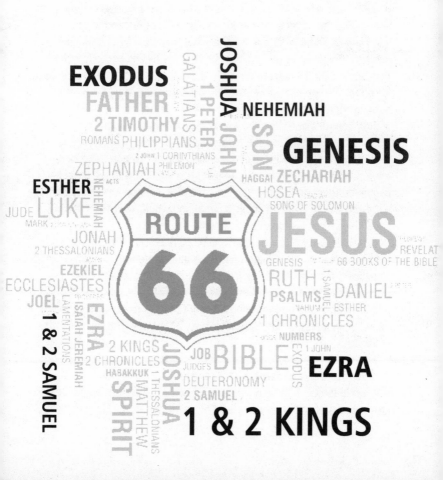

# Day 1: **The ride of our lives**

Luke is funny. He is clever. He is 145 cm tall and has brown eyes.

What is your mental image of Luke from that description? Are you imagining a small clown turning cartwheels? Are you thinking geeky and peculiar? Awkward and studious? Scheming and tricking? I'm afraid all of these are way off mark. Describing anyone in terms of a few physical features and personality traits falls seriously short. So let me introduce you to my son Luke another way – with a story.

Yesterday Luke brought his schoolwork home. When we asked why he hadn't completed the work at school, he explained crossly that he had been waiting in the queue to get the materials from the teacher when he saw one of his friends struggling. He went over to help him out and rejoined the queue. Just as he was almost at the front he spotted a girl crying, so he went over to give her a hand and by the time he rejoined the queue again, she was smiling. By the end of the lesson he had helped half the class in one way or another, but had hardly started his project. When his teacher saw his work, she told him off for "doing nothing" and gave him a warning.

Just from this one short story, we gain an insight into the way Luke relates to others, his selflessness, and his sense of justice. We read "clever" as mentally resourceful, and "funny" as good at making other people smile. But more than just picturing him, you are probably beginning to relate to Luke. You may even have begun to think about what you would do in his shoes or what you would say to him if you were his teacher, his friend or his parent.

Statements like "Luke is 145 cm tall" are important. But they are merely the bones of a skeleton when it comes to getting to know somebody. A story fleshes out the description, giving us a clearer picture of the person, and offering us the possibility of intimacy and relationship. When God introduces himself to us in the beginning of the Bible, he does so through story after story after story. This has a number of effects:

## 1. Stories reveal God's character[12]
Not just in terms of abstract concepts that could be misconstrued, but also in terms of concrete examples. For the most part the story of the

12  See Newbigin, L., 1989, *The Gospel in a Pluralist Society*, SPCK, p. 99.

Bible is a retelling of how God has connected characters, communities, continents and the cosmos itself in his great big story for all of creation, making the character of the invisible God visible to us.

## 2. Stories draw us into the story

Stories abduct our emotions, stealing them away into the drama as we recognize the dilemmas and empathize with the characters.[13] By experiencing the stories God has given us in this way, our imagination, our ambition and our lives are drawn into the captivating narrative of the Bible.

## 3. Stories draw us into relationship

As we see God's character in action, we get to know different aspects of his personality and foundations for a relationship are built as we share his hopes and heartaches.

## 4. Stories make us who we are

"In order to make sense of our lives and to make our most important decisions, we depend on some story."[14] In a world of competing stories the Bible tells us true stories about the way things really happened so that we can be caught up into God's ultimate story of the grand sweep of history. Sometimes we zoom in and see the fine detail – like in the story of Joseph and his jealous brothers. Other times we zoom out to see the genealogies that summarize generations of stories where God was faithful to his people. It has been said that history is "His Story", but it is also our story, as we too belong somewhere in the sweep of history described between Genesis 1 and Revelation 22.

## 5. Stories change our lives

One sweltering summer's day my wife and I heard a story about a beautiful newborn baby girl who had no home to go to, as her birth mother was unable to care for her. She was lying in the hospital that hot afternoon, oblivious to the uncertainties of her future as social workers phoned around possible placements. We were newly approved foster carers. On hearing this story we faced a choice. Our decision to get

---

13   See Sweet, L., McLaren, B. D. & Haselmayer, J., 2003, *A is for Abductive: The Language of the Emerging Church*, Zondervan, pp. 31–33.
14   See Bartholomew, C. & Goheen, M., 2006, *The Drama of Scripture: Finding our place in the biblical story*, SPCK, p. 1. Reproduced with permission of The Licensor through PLSClear.

involved in the story of this little girl had life-changing consequences as we first fostered her, then adopted her, loving her as our own daughter. Reading the stories of the Old Testament comes with a health warning: the more we get to know God, and the more we get drawn into the Bible story, the harder it will be to ignore the invitation to join the ride of our lives in God's big plan for the universe.

### TRAVEL JOURNAL: Genesis 1:1–31

1. God is introduced as the lead character in the story of the Bible. How does this story seek to inspire awe in you as you read?
   (See verses 1, 3 and 16.)

2. The story of the beginning of the universe is told with great artistry. Where do you notice repetitions, poetry or unusual turns of phrase?

3. The hinge-point of the story seems to be the creation of human beings (verses 27–31). Find four differences compared to the rest of creation. Why are they significant?

4. Use the five points about how stories help us to engage with Genesis 1. How does this story:

⊕ reveal God's character?

⊕ draw us into relationship?

⊕ draw us into the story?

⊕ make us who we are?

⊕ change our lives?

# Day 2: **Mirror, signal, manoeuvre**

Of the 4,000 or more volumes that my wife and I own, there is one that I particularly treasure. It is one of my smallest and scruffiest books and even the letters on its spine have been rubbed away. But every time I see it, I remember the romance of a day twenty years earlier. I was in Shakespeare's Stratford with my soon-to-be fiancée when we discovered this compact copy of *Romeo and Juliet* in a second-hand shop. Sitting by the river in view of the Swan Theatre, I gave that book as a farewell present to my girlfriend as she left to spend a year working in Germany. Somehow we survived the long-distance relationship and that copy of *Romeo and Juliet* now sits on our shelf reminding us of young love, of the pain of separation, and of the hope of return.

If I were to tell you that some recent visitors to my home spotted that famous romantic tragedy on my bookshelf, and had never heard of it before, I guess you would be surprised. But imagine your shock if I then added that I could summarize the play in just thirteen words:

- ⊕  Hate destroys families.

- ⊕  Love is stronger than hate.

- ⊕  Love is stronger than death.

The statements are true enough, but the story has been stripped of its plot, its suspense, its beauty, its emotions, its characters, and its context. My summary may have left my visitors a little more informed, but I doubt I would have inspired them to go away and discover the play for themselves.

Many of the sermons I hear, and even many I have preached, easily end up as a bland set of bullet-points, often handily beginning with the same letter! For example, you could go away from a sermon based on the story of the call of Abraham in Genesis 12 with these lessons:

- ⊕  God is patient.

- ⊕  God is generous.

- ⊕  God is missionary.

Here are three true statements,[15] but the Bible passage, which started out as a story, has ended up as systematic theology. This is as dissatisfying as going into a restaurant and ordering their best soup, and being given instead a list of the ingredients. Or visiting the Louvre to see a Renaissance masterpiece, only to discover that scientists had immortalized the exhibits by distilling the paints into test-tubes arranged in alphabetical order of their chemical composition. Sometimes we are in danger of reducing the Bible so much, that although we may find a truth, we lose the sensation and the impact that the story was supposed to produce.[16]

It is the basic assumption in this book that God in his wisdom inspired the Scriptures and gave us just the kind of book that we needed. It is no accident or mistake that God inspired so much of the Bible to be in story form and preserved those stories over the millennia so they would be handed down in the format we see in front of us. Of course God could have sent us bullet-points instead, but he chose not to. God's aim was not that we boil these stories down to their bare minimum ingredients. God's aim was the opposite – that the stories could boil over into the messy reality of our lives.

In order to understand *Romeo and Juliet*, we need to understand the language and the culture that Shakespeare was writing in. But that tragic play set in the fifteenth century, with its rigid conventions of marriage, still has an impact in our more liberal society. The stories of the Bible are not human works of fiction, like Shakespearean plays, but divine accounts of history and therefore have endless potential to impact our own lives. Nevertheless, we still need to acknowledge the presence of the two worlds, whichever part of the Bible narrative we are reading: the world of the Bible text with its language, culture and time in history, and our world with its very different language, culture and time in history.[17] The following tool of narrative Bible study is adapted from that vital all-terrain habit I learned in my driving lessons: "Mirror, Signal, Manoeuvre".

---

15   Kevin Vanhoozer puts it well: "The gospel is informative: 'he is risen.' Without some propositional core, the church would lose its *raison d'être*, leaving only programs and pot-lucks. At the same time, to reduce the truth of Scripture to a set of propositions is unnecessarily reductionist." Vanhoozer, K., 2005, "Lost in Interpretation? Truth, Scripture and Hermeneutics", *Journal of the Evangelical Theological Society*, 48/1, March 2005, p. 100.
16   For more on this theme see Arthurs, J. D., 2007, *Preaching with Variety: How to Recreate the Dynamics of Biblical Genres*, Kregel.
17   Stott, J., 1998, *I Believe in Preaching*, Hodder & Stoughton.

⊕ **MIRROR:** Look back and try to understand how the original audience would have experienced the Bible passage.

⊕ **SIGNAL:** Ask God to help you to understand the passage's significance today. How is the story used elsewhere in the Bible? How does the story set the course for our lives today?

⊕ **MANOEUVRE:** What are you going to do now to change your actions, attitude or understanding as a result of this Bible passage?

Looking back to what a story meant to its first hearers before we look to our own situation may take some getting used to. However awkward and time-consuming it may feel to first look back, and then look around before looking forward, this art of time travel will protect us from the dangers of misapplying the Bible, and will resource us to move forward confidently.

**TRAVEL JOURNAL: Genesis 12:1–9**

1. Flick back through chapters 9–12. What do we learn about the world as Abram saw it? How do you imagine Abram felt about God's call in verse 1, and the promises in verses 2–3 and 7? From Abram's perspective, how does the story work out for him? (Scan through Genesis 12–25.)

2. How does Abram's call set the direction for how we understand the life of faith? (See Galatians 3 and Romans 4.)

3. Ultimately God's promise will be fulfilled at the end of time. How is Abram's call therefore still applicable to those of us who are his spiritual descendants? (See especially Genesis 12:2–3.)

4. How does Hebrews 11:8–12 help us to live out this story? What are you going to do about this?

# Day 3: **One eye on the road**

Giants, gluttons, goldsmiths, grape-pickers, gaolers, governors and grandparents – the Bible has them all, and more. With 2,930 different characters scattered through 66 books, it is easy to see why the most popular way of handling Old Testament stories is to do character-based studies. David is a prime example. It is an amazing story of rags to riches to rebellion to restoration. It is ripe picking for a sermon series or a Sunday school class because the story is so gripping, especially the classic confrontation between David and Goliath. The poor little delivery boy bringing cheese takeaway to his brothers on the front line gets drawn into the public humiliation of the Israelites by the giant's taunts. Using the simple tools of his trade, David rises to the challenge, creates the first guided missile and proves that the bigger they come, the harder they fall.

The Sunday school version of this lesson often finishes like this. "Don't worry about bullies like Goliath the giant. Be courageous and faithful like David the giant-killer. Whatever troubles you face, however big they seem, with God's power on your side nothing is impossible and you will see victory in your lives."

The story is fantastic, but this application is faulty on several fronts, because using the characters of the Bible in this way to navigate life actually poses more problems than it solves.

The main problem is that when we focus on a Bible character, we naturally try to draw parallels between that person and our own lives. Because we are biased, we like to identify with the "hero" characters like David, Abraham, Moses, Deborah and Jesus, while the "villain" characters like Goliath or the Pharisees we apply to other people – usually people we don't like. There are lots of instances in history of Christians misinterpreting Scripture in this way. The Afrikaans church in South Africa during apartheid, for example, called themselves the people of God and dismissed the Africans, equating them with the Canaanites who should be ejected from the land.

By identifying ourselves with the Bible heroes we read about, it is easy for those human characters to become caricatures and for us to turn the real hero, God, into a mere bystander. The Bible employs biblical characters "not as ethical models, nor as heroes for emulation, or examples for warning, but as people whose story has been taken up into the Bible in order to reveal what God is doing for and through them".[18] This is the way that the Hall of Fame in Hebrews 11 describes the Old Testament characters, reminding us of their human, not hero, status and drawing us back to our common story:[19] "God had planned something better for us so that only together with us would they be made perfect."[20]

The third danger of character-based Bible study is that we can turn a one-off outcome into a general promise. From the David and Goliath story it would be great to assume that we will always see victory in impossible situations if we rely on God. But from other incidents in David's life, we see that this is not always the case.[21] The Bible as a whole teaches us that although God promises to be with us and help us in every circumstance, and ultimately bring us safely into eternal life, he does not promise to deliver us from every trouble we face in this life. Misreading the Bible could lead us to false hope and the disappointments that send us running from God instead of to him.

The final and most important danger of focusing on characters is that we forget to read the Bible with Jesus in mind. Graeme Goldsworthy[22] helpfully shows that even within the David and Goliath episode there are important signposts to Jesus: David is an errand boy who has been secretly anointed king of Israel by Samuel the prophet, but when faced with a mighty enemy, God's people send this servant king to fight on their behalf. He is their substitute who, in his weakness, relies on God to defeat the threat. This story reminds us of the battle faced by Jesus, the "Son of David", on the cross. From this perspective we recognize God as the hero, Jesus as our Saviour, and we ourselves identify with the fearful Israelites quivering at the sound of Goliath's voice, too afraid to rely on God, but saved anyway by the Lord's anointed.

There's a 100-metre stretch of road in Wiltshire where for a moment you can glimpse one of the oldest landmarks in the world – Stonehenge. I am sure many accidents would occur at the point where this world-famous historic site suddenly appears on the horizon, if it were not for the number of tractors and caravans that slow that carriageway down!

---

18   Greidanus, S., 1988, *The Modern Preacher and the Ancient Text*, IVP, p. 118.
19   Hebrews 11 begins and ends with us. Verse 3 says: "By faith, we…" and verses 39–40 say: "These were all commended for their faith, yet none of them received what had been promised, since God had planned something better for us so that only together with us would they be made perfect."
20   Hebrews 11:40.
21   See Psalm 13, for example.
22   Goldsworthy, G., 1994, *Gospel and Kingdom: A Christian Interpretation of the Old Testament*, Paternoster, p. 26.

When I drive that way I try to keep one eye on the road, and one eye on the horizon for that ancient circle of stones. Similarly, as we travel through the Old Testament, we focus on the narrative in front of us, but we will also see glimpses of Jesus on the horizon. By ensuring that God is the hero of every story, we are better prepared to understand what we can learn from the other 2,930 characters of the Bible.

### TRAVEL JOURNAL: 1 Samuel 17:1–58

1. What do we already know about Saul, David and Goliath? Think about what is at stake for each of them in the stand-off described in verses 1–11.

2. In what ways does this passage underline David as an unlikely hero? Look at the way the other characters in the story relate to him.

3. In Matthew 1:1 and Luke 18:3 Jesus is called the "Son of David". How does seeing David – the anointed shepherd-saviour – as a snapshot of Jesus help us to appreciate the significance of this story at another level?

4. If David gives us a picture of Jesus in this story, who then are we supposed to relate to? What is the primary lesson we should learn?

# Day 4: **Signposts**

There's a classic story about a little boy who is asked in church: "What is grey, has a bushy tail and collects nuts for the winter?" The little boy reluctantly puts his hand up and says, "I know the answer is always Jesus, but that really sounds like a squirrel to me." Having seen in the last chapter that the Old Testament is full of glimpses of Jesus, we now need to make sure that we find him in the right places.[23]

Sometimes we need to understand when a squirrel is just a squirrel.

For example, there is a really short story in 2 Samuel 23:20 which tells us simply that "Benaiah… went down into a pit on a snowy day and killed a lion." The brief story illustrates the reputation and prowess of King Solomon's chief military general at a time when God's people were dealing with numerous boundary disputes and power struggles. However, some Christians have taken this story to another level, and interpreted it as follows: "Benaiah represents Jesus as the hero of the story, the lion represents the devil, prowling around looking for whom he may devour, and the pit represents our sinful world." They go on to explain that this verse means that Jesus came down from heaven into our pit, and defeated the devil.

One scholar called this kind of approach "illegitimate totality transfer".[24] Just because a word is used in one context in a certain way doesn't mean it carries with it the totality of that meaning in another context. It is not hard to see why we get so easily confused. The image of a lion is used in the Bible not only to describe the devil,[25] but also to describe God[26] and Jesus.[27]

So how do we know when the stories of the Old Testament are signposts that point to Jesus, and when lions and squirrels are just lions and squirrels? In the story of Esther, for example, are we supposed to be reminded of Jesus when Mordecai refuses to bow down to the wicked Haman, or when Esther risks her life for the sake of her people, or when Haman is hoisted up high to be executed?

The following tool helps us not to lose the plot by showing us how to

---

23   A very helpful book on this subject, which is sometimes known as "typology", is Clowney, E. P., 1988, *The Unfolding Mystery: Discovering Christ in the Old Testament*, IVP.
24   See Osborne, G. R., 1991, *The Hermeneutical Spiral*, IVP, p. 66, citing Barr, J., 1961, *The Semantics of Biblical Language*, Oxford University Press, p. 218.
25   1 Peter 5:8.
26   Amos 1:2.
27   Revelation 5:5.

**31**

discover for ourselves how the story should be seen with the advantage of New Testament hindsight. Let us take a closer look at the book of Esther, at first glance a rags-to-riches fairy tale where the faithful foster father wins the king's favour and the villain gets humiliated and hanged.

## P = Perspective: who is telling the story and why?

God has inspired biblical storytellers to help us see the events of history from a God-centred perspective. This is clear in the book of Esther, even though God is not mentioned. It might help to imagine God as the film director who is behind the cameras ensuring that the plot weaves together under his control. Exploring the perspective of the storyteller will involve looking at the intended audience, and finding which bits of the story are significant, and which are incidental. We see in the example of Esther that the ethical problems in the story (forced sex, arranged marriage, the death penalty and polygamy) are presented as background facts of the story with no moral judgment on the part of the author – these are not what we should be focusing on. The overall purpose of the book is to celebrate the averted genocide of the Jewish people.

## L = Layers: how do the story layers overlap?

There are multiple layers in every story told in the Bible. Each story fits within the specific book, within a specific historical and geographical context, within the big story of God's dealings with his people, and in the light of Christ's coming. The impending genocide leads Esther to a dilemma, which should be read in the light of the author's account in chapter 1 of the fate of her predecessor, Queen Vashti, when she challenged the king's absolute power. It should be read in the light of God's unbreakable covenant promise to Abraham, repeated through the generations, that God would bless his people and they would bless the nations. And it should be read in the light of Jesus' willingness to go as a lamb to the slaughter for the sake of his people. The cost was high, but Esther's decision to risk her own life for others not only points to Jesus, but also acts as a signpost in our own lives, pointing us to make decisions to put others first.

## O = Organization: which aspect of the story is highlighted?

Storytellers have lots of tools to help us know which are the important bits. They can use pace, symmetry, language and repetition to underline key points. In Esther we see the story beginning and ending with three banquets[28] – and the unlikely displacing of power in each one. Although God is not specifically mentioned, there can be no doubt that this storyteller clearly recognizes God, not King Xerxes, as the one in full control of the fate of his people.

## T = Tension: what are the uncomfortable aspects of the story?

Often the story will balance on a key event, decision or conversation. To find this hinge-point, imagine where you would pause the story for that cliff-hanger ending that would make everyone want to tune in to the next episode. The book of Esther centres on her decision to speak up for her people. This suspense is mirrored when Jesus – also facing a death sentence – weighs up the consequences of his life-and-death dilemma to go forward as our substitute in the garden of Gethsemane.

Seeing Jesus in the Old Testament is not just imaginative wishful thinking, like seeing his silhouette on a grilled-cheese sandwich. God really wants the stories to switch on flashing neon signs in our minds, pointing to Jesus when Joseph is wrongly punished, when Moses feeds the hungry thousands, or when Jesse's youngest and shortest son is picked out as Israel's future king. These stories help us not to lose the plot in our own lives when we feel unfairly treated, insufficiently resourced or simply unnoticed.

---

28  See Firth, D. G., 2009, *The Message of Esther: God present but unseen*, IVP, for a user-friendly analysis.

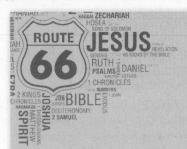

### TRAVEL JOURNAL: Esther 4:1–17

1. The Jews are a tiny minority facing extermination from a pagan government, and God seems silent. How might this story correspond or contrast with our own context?

2. How does knowing God's promises to the Jewish people help us understand the wider significance of this story?

3. The story of Esther begins and ends with feasts, but here Esther calls a three-day fast (verse 16). What might be the significance of a fast at the pivot-point of this book?

4. How does the author underline the tension in this story? How does this chapter compare with Jesus' moment of crisis in the garden of Gethsemane? How do these stories cause you to think differently about dilemmas you are facing?

# Day 5: **Which way now?**

He stood out watching the sunset and in the distance he could see the silhouette of the mountains that contained the Kosovan border. In a few years' time over 400,000 refugees would pour over that border into his small, poor, rural town, transforming its reputation from feuding and thieving and blood revenge to a refuge worthy of its nomination for the Nobel peace prize. One day he would have to decide what he would sacrifice in order to offer the help they would so desperately need. But for now he faced a lesser decision, and he was asking God – not Allah, as his family had taught him in the past – for guidance. He remembered the preacher had told the story of Gideon at church that week and decided he would leave his precious sheepskin coat outside his front door so that God could tell him which way his decision should go.

I would love to finish this story the way this young Christian was anticipating: dry coat, wet ground, God's will discerned, decision made. But what happened next was sadly predictable, as well as being a costly and painful lesson in misapplying the Bible. He opened the door the next morning and the coat was gone – missing, presumed stolen – never to be seen again.

When we turn to our Bibles, it is often because we are looking for help for a specific need. We have a difficult decision to make, we need comfort in an adversity we are facing, we need a spiritual boost, or we need a glimmer of hope. Although the Bible never promises us any quick-fix solutions, we are still disappointed when we don't find one.

Six hundred years before the birth of Jesus lived another storyteller. He was a slave in Greece, but his stories have outlived the names or the works of his masters. He told stories about a slow hare and a quick tortoise, about a heroic mouse and a helpless lion and many others with important moral lessons about values such as honesty, honour, and hard work.

In our search for a quick fix, it is often tempting to read the Bible in the same way that we might read one of Aesop's fables, looking for the neat moral lesson for the day or something that we can put into immediate practice. This may be the way we were taught the Bible as children. Perhaps it is because we preachers find it hard to resist moralizing when we look out at our congregation and catch the eye of somebody who we know is not pulling their weight in their home, work or church life. It may be because we have not yet taken in God's gospel of grace and are still looking for ways to measure up. Or it may be because when a quick-fix culture meets the struggle of investing in the difficult daily discipline of personal Bible reading, we feel dissatisfied unless we can extract some instant lesson to apply for the day ahead.

The boy who cried wolf, for example, is attributed to Aesop and is an easy story to grasp. It has a neat and satisfying, albeit grisly, moral outcome when the boy who has lied to the village gets his just desserts as a tasty dessert for the wolf. If we read the Bible stories in this way, then we get into trouble. The story of Ruth would be reduced to "be nice to the mother-in-law", come what may. And the account of Jacob, the mummy's boy who lied to his father on his deathbed, could lead to any number of moral lessons depending on our mood – honour your mother, not your father; God helps those who help themselves; flight is better than fight; you can't trust anyone; cheat by name, cheat by nature; you don't ask, you don't get. All these may seem very satisfying, but in the long run, they don't allow us to reflect God's character. Ruth and Jacob are not in the Bible to help us justify manipulating our parents or emigrating with our in-laws.

Although we may enjoy the moral victories of Sisera's gory tent-peg,[29] Daniel's vegetarian diet,[30] or fat Eglon's fate,[31] there are lots of passages of the Bible that don't fit a tidy moral pattern. In fact, the Bible is filled with moral misfits like Moses who got away with murder, or Judge Jephthah who stupidly sacrificed his own daughter in an attempt to appease God; or the war hero Gideon who spent his veteran years in idolatry. From the patriarchs to the prophets to the disciples and deacons, the sting in the tale is that there often is no sting in the tale. The whole Bible is full of stories of bad people who get right with God and good people who don't. The Bible doesn't supply the simple and swift satisfactory conclusion of an Aesop's tale – so we must learn to read the Bible with patience.

When I go shopping in a supermarket, my bill at the checkout can vary enormously depending on how hungry I am. My most expensive time is around 5 p.m. when I pile a whole load of irresistible snack foods into the trolley to keep me going on the way home, and a salt-laden, preservative-packed Indian takeaway box that could be sizzling hot two minutes after it meets my microwave somehow appears at the checkout!

---

29  Judges 4.
30  Daniel 1.
31  Judges 3.

Packets of flour, vegetables and eggs, on the other hand, have no appeal – what's the fun of nibbling on those? But in the long term, it is those ingredients that are going to provide what I need.

In the same way, we often come to the Bible spiritually peckish, and satisfy ourselves temporarily on some unhealthy takeaway moral. But what we need is the raw materials for the healthy long-term diet God wants to feed us with, packed with invisible vitamins and minerals that will make us spiritually strong.

However urgently I feel I need guidance, the story of Gideon is not a model for overnight decision-making! But as we turn to look at the other genres of the Bible, we will see that the narrative literature alongside the other writing styles are like building blocks that together form an infrastructure for a biblical way of thinking. Decision-making in the long run will be far easier than risking the theft of the fleece on your doorstep. As we get to know God's character from the Old Testament, his revelation in Jesus, his principles of living from the law and the wisdom literature, and how to live now in light of the future as explained in Revelation, godly decision-making will become more and more second nature.

**TRAVEL JOURNAL: Genesis 27:1–46**

1. In Genesis 25, God tells Rebekah that her younger twin will be served by the older twin, and later in that chapter Esau sells his birthright for a bowl of soup. Why do you think Rebekah and Jacob take matters into their own hands here to ensure Jacob's dominance?

2. How does their quick-fix plan pay off and/or backfire?

3. Read Genesis 29. What painful means does God use to teach Jacob to be patient and take the long view?

4. What does it mean for us to take the long view – with our Bible-reading, with trusting God's promises or in our home and work life?

## Small Group Study 1
# Living faithfully with the narrative

Draw a graph that describes your own sense of spiritual well-being over the last five years, filling in the dates along the bottom of the graph. When have the peaks and troughs occurred?

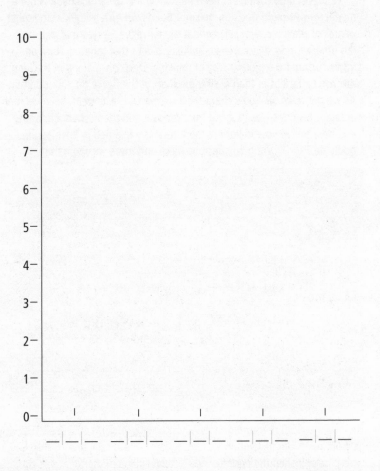

The book of Judges is structured on a pattern of peaks and troughs that described the people of Israel's relationship with God. Use the passages indicated to fill in the boxes below for Gideon.

| | Othniel | Deborah | Gideon |
|---|---|---|---|
| Rebellion | Judges 3:7: "The Israelites did evil in the eyes of the LORD…" | Judges 4:1: "the Israelites once again did evil in the eyes of the LORD." | Judges 6:1: |
| Retribution | Judges 3:8: "The anger of the LORD burned against Israel so that he sold them into the hands of Cushan-Rishathaim…" | Judges 4:2: "So the LORD sold them into the hands of Jabin, a king of Canaan…" | Judges 6:2–6: |
| Repentance | Judges 3:9: "But when they cried out to the LORD…" | Judges 4:3: "the Israelites… cried to the LORD for help." | Judges 6:7: |
| Rescue | Judges 3:9: "he raised up for them a deliverer, Othniel…" | Judges 4:4: "Deborah, a prophetess… was leading Israel at that time." | Judges 6:8 – 7:25: |
| Rest | Judges 3:11: "the land had peace for forty years…" | Judges 5:31: "the land had peace for forty years." | Judges 8:28: |

There is a cyclical pattern throughout the book of Judges as the people go from rebellion, to retribution, to repentance, to rescue and to rest. But when they reached the period of rest, it was only a matter of time before they decided to rebel again.

# The Cycle in Judges

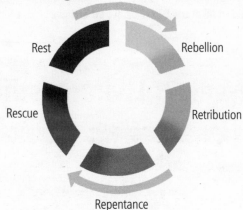

Rest

Rebellion

Rescue

Retribution

Repentance

⊕ Think of examples of how this same kind of pattern occurs in other parts of the Bible or in your own life.

⊕ Does your life at the moment feel like it fits into one of the segments on the diagram? What does the story of Judges inspire you to pray for in this circumstance?

⊕ Do you think your church is in one of those segments? What does the structure of the book of Judges inspire you to pray for your church?

⊕ The last verse in the book of Judges says: "In those days Israel had no king; everyone did as he saw fit." Why is this such a sad end to this book? To what extent are we still in this dire situation today?

⊕ Living faithfully as we wait for the return of King Jesus, who will bring in the perfect, permanent rest of peace with God, is the opposite of living egotistically and individualistically. How can the book of Judges and the Old Testament narratives help us to live faithfully, both individually and as a church, in the meantime?

# Week 2: **Living distinctively**

*The law and its application to life*

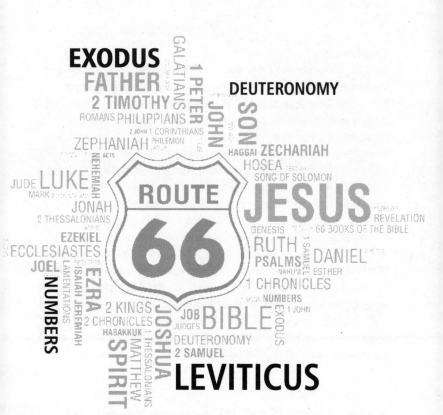

# Day 1: **White lines**

It was a strange suggestion. All around me was the beautiful unspoiled countryside of Georgia, and yet my host was asking me to roll a can of fizzy drink down the hill. It was a long steep hill, and I really did not fancy running down it in the heat to collect the can again at the bottom. But after I glanced around furtively to make sure nobody was watching me, I obediently dropped it out of the car door. As I did so I had the shock of my life. The can rolled up the hill! I rubbed my eyes. I checked the can. I tried again – up the hill it went. As a science student, I deduced that there must be some weird electromagnetic phenomenon at work, and grabbed a glass bottle from the car. But the bottle went up the hill too. Finally, to silence my scepticism, my host shut the car engine down, took off the handbrake and together we watched the car coast uphill!

### Confusion

The optical illusion that I saw that day seemed to turn everything I had learned about gravity on its head. In a similar way, many people who know their New Testament and its teaching on salvation by grace, find it difficult when they come to the Old Testament law which seems to teach the opposite – that God sets impossible moral and practical standards and withholds his love until they are met. But sometimes what we think we see is not what is really there. Do the books of the law really present a God who hadn't come up with the idea of grace yet? Was God rather like a mean-spirited father who won't hug his son unless he gets full marks in an algebra test? Appearances can be deceptive.

This week we will take a closer look at the often neglected books of the Old Testament law. Today we will begin by exploding the myth that God is some grumpy deity in the Old Testament who lightens up in the New Testament.[32] God did not change his mind or his character or his plans when it came to something as important as how people have their sins forgiven and enter into a life-transforming, world-transforming relationship with him. Let's get straight to the heart of the issue – the jewel in the crown of the Old Testament laws – the Ten Commandments.

---

32  For a fuller exploration of this theme see Holwerda, D. E., 1995, *Jesus and Israel: One Covenant or Two?*, IVP.

## Context

If any part of the Bible could take the prize for "most holy", the Ten Commandments would have fair claim to it, with their unique assertion that they were "inscribed by the finger of God".[33] Of course, we are assured that all Scripture is "God-breathed",[34] so this doesn't make the Ten Commandments any more trustworthy than the rest of the Bible. However, this passage is highlighted as an important summary of the Old Testament laws.

In the introduction to the Ten Commandments in Exodus 20, we are given a major indicator to help us understand the purpose of the law:

> And God spoke all these words: "I am the LORD your God, who brought you out of Egypt, out of the land of slavery."[35]

Before he explains his laws to his people, God wants to remind them that these words are to be read in the context of his powerful, loving, and historic acts, and in the light of his eternal, unchanging, "I am" character. God is not like a harsh headmaster laying down the ground rules on the first day of school. He is more like the kind lifeguard who has just rescued a drowning man and is now telling him to kick off his shoes, don't thrash about, and don't panic.

## Continuum

The order of events is very important. God could have given his people the laws while they were in slavery and asked them to earn their right to be rescued. But God saves his people first – by grace, and then shows them how to live consistently and distinctively as his people. As Old Testament scholar Alec Motyer puts it, "what the Lord *does* precedes what the Lord *demands*".[36]

## Consistency

There is no room here to think that the Bible ever suggests that we are saved by our own efforts. Understanding that the laws are given in the context of grace, after God's people have already been freely rescued, is liberating for us too. All too often we live as if we are saved by our

---

33   Exodus 31:18.
34   2 Timothy 3:16–17.
35   Exodus 20:1–2.
36   Motyer, A., 1996, *Look to the Rock: An Old Testament background to our understanding of Christ*, IVP, p. 39.

ability to live up to God's moral standards. But consistently through the whole Bible, even in the Old Testament law, we are reminded that there is nothing we can do that will make God love us more.

## Content

Often the clash of cultures between the world of the Bible and our contemporary situation makes it very difficult for us to see the significance or relevance of the multitude of Old Testament laws. But here in the Ten Commandments we find a fixed point to help any community live in peace with each other and with God.

The fact that the law brought freedom is no optical illusion – just a change of perspective. Imagine two drivers. One is driving in good visibility and curses the restrictiveness of the white lines on the road – she feels disgruntled that they tell her not to overtake, not to speed, and not to park. Another driver has to drive through heavy fog. For him the white lines are his lifeline – they show him which direction to take, how close he is to a junction, how to stay in the right part of the road to avoid accidents, and where children are most likely to be playing. We can often have the perspective of the first driver, and can only see God's laws like the restrictive white lines, or worse, like the speed cameras waiting to catch us out when we least expect it. But to the people of Israel they were a lifeline, and the whole Bible pays tribute to the law as a treasured gift of grace.[37]

---

37   John 1:16–17: "From the fullness of his grace we have all received one blessing after another. For the law was given through Moses; grace and truth came through Jesus Christ."

**TRAVEL JOURNAL: Exodus 20:1–21**

1. If your eleven-year-old neighbour was about to go to secondary school and asked you for a list of do's and don'ts for getting the most out of it, what would you say? What would motivate your advice? How does this help us understand the Ten Commandments?

2. How does reading the Ten Commandments in the light of the gracious rescue of God (verses 1–2) change our perspective on them? How can they be understood to be a gift from God to his people?

3. Divide the Ten Commandments up into the following two categories: Relationship with God, and Relationship with Others. How does this provide a strong framework for living distinctively as God's people?

4. The two categories overlap at the fourth commandment. Why do you think there is such a long explanation of the Sabbath commandment compared to the others? How does the reason for keeping the Sabbath in Exodus 20 compare with the restatement of the law in Deuteronomy 5:15? How does it show consistency with Jesus' teaching in Mark 2:23 – 3:5?

# Day 2: **Right-hand drive**

I may well have sold my soul on the Internet. As I very rarely read the fine print when shopping online, it would not surprise me to find out that I could have been one of the 7,500 people who unwittingly sold their souls to a computer games store after failing to read the website-based terms and conditions. Online retailer GameStation sneakily inserted the "immortal soul clause" into the conditions that shoppers had to agree to when making an online purchase. Their publicity stunt highlighted the fact that some 90 per cent of us fail to read the fine print.

The law sections of the Bible feel like the fine print, which may suit that 10 per cent of people who care about such things, but the rest of us seem to get on with our Christian life happily ignoring it. Occasionally we may resolve to read the Bible through from cover to cover and get as far as Leviticus 3, but at that point our determination melts away and we re-resolve to try again next year.

There is no doubt this is a difficult part of the Bible. There are over 600 commandments in Exodus, Numbers, Leviticus and Deuteronomy and it is very hard for modern readers of the Bible to understand them, let alone know how to apply them. The sense of dislocation from these parts of the Bible affects us on several levels.

*Stylistic dislocation.* Just like the legal wording of the fine print of an online contract, the meticulous lists of stipulations contained in parts of Exodus and Deuteronomy, not to mention the whole of Leviticus, can be extremely intimidating. The laws often feel impenetrably unreadable.

*Historical dislocation.* Tablet computers, air travel and biotechnology seem a million miles away and a million years away from the problems of waving sheaves, coveting manservants or sacrificing animals. The laws often feel ridiculously irrelevant.

*Theological dislocation.* The events of the New Testament changed the way we relate to God, and many of the Old Testament laws no longer need to be practised. We know that we don't need to follow the food laws (Acts 10) and we are pretty sure we don't need to sacrifice animals (Hebrews 10). But should we follow laws regarding cancelling debts or creating cities of refuge or cleansing from mildew? The laws often feel randomly irrational.

Ironically, the dislocation we feel can actually help us to study the Bible better. The awkwardness I feel driving on the other side of the road in mainland Europe means that I am far more alert at roundabouts and junctions and motorways than I am on home territory in the UK. Everything I do is deliberate, and I consciously check and double-check my mirrors to ensure that I am driving as safely as possible. In a similar way, we can use these dislocations when we come to the law to go deeper in our relationship with God by finding him in unfamiliar territory.

Take, for example, Deuteronomy 15:12–18, a paragraph dedicated to the hiring and firing of Hebrew slaves. It can easily appear impenetrable, irrelevant, and irrational. But the difficulties of reading the passage can simply be turned into a tool for a deeper engagement with the passage.

*Stylistic dislocation.* These verses probably bear very little resemblance to your own employment contract! But there may be some similarities; they probably both involve length of contract, remuneration and perks. Looking more closely at the differences, we see that God's instructions to an employer are based on God's rescue, generosity and respect. These values would have marked out the Jewish nation's treatment of slaves from the norms of the nations around them, and could also be seen as countercultural today.

*Historical dislocation.* At first glance it may appear that God is sanctioning slavery in these verses. In the light of history, we struggle with this, as we equate slavery with kidnapping, forced labour and the denial of basic human rights. Christians quite rightly were instrumental in ending the cruel cross-Atlantic slave trade of the eighteenth century, and continue to fight against people-trafficking for the sex-slave trade today. In stark contrast, slavery in the Old Testament seems to be a way of helping those who have ended up in poverty, by incorporating them into an extended family situation in return for work. As Christians in today's unequal world, we cannot try to keep the poor at arm's length, but we try to work out how we follow the cues of the Old Testament law to empower the poor without paternalistic patronizing. Tim Keller puts it like this: "the inevitable sign that you know you are a sinner saved by sheer, costly grace is a sensitive social conscience and a life poured out in deeds of sheer service to the poor".[38]

*Theological dislocation.* Theologically we might struggle with the concepts of slavery and freedom. The challenge is not to compare this legal code with our own day and age but to see it within the context of the wider story of the Bible. Generosity toward the needy, relationships

---

38  Keller, T., *The Prodigal God*, Hodder & Stoughton, p. 112.

marked primarily by love and respect, families united because of God's grace and rescue – these are the strong themes that resound here, as throughout the Bible. Here is where we can apply these values more directly to our context.

### TRAVEL JOURNAL: Deuteronomy 15

1. What is God teaching us about himself through these laws?
2. God reminds the Jewish people of their own experience of slavery. How can our difficult experiences and our experiences of God's mercy help us in the way we treat people around us today? (See 2 Corinthians 1:1–7.)
3. Many people take the sentence "the LORD your God will bless you in all your work and in everything you put your hand to" (verse 10) out of its context to claim that God desires prosperity for all Christians. What do we learn about "blessing" from this chapter that might challenge that idea?
4. How do you explain the apparent contradiction between verses 4 and 11? What big themes from this chapter can help us to know how to treat people suffering in poverty around us? How are these being shown in your own life and the life of your church?

# Day 3: **Map upgrade**

It seemed completely out of place. The perfect house, complete with hanging baskets and precisely symmetrical curtains, sat in an enormous expanse of rubble, machinery, mud and scaffolding, without a streetlamp or road name in sight. The visitors, wearing waterproof boots and hard hats, walked into a spotless hallway, a state-of-the-art kitchen and an immaculate magazine-picture lounge. The developer had finished this one brand-new house to the last detail as a show-home to inspire potential buyers as to the quality of build he was planning for the other houses on the building site. Of course, the other houses would differ greatly in layout, décor and size, but many of the distinctive features would be carried over into all the properties, and so the worked example was the best way to reel in the buyers, whatever their requirements.

The laws of the Old Testament function in a similar way to that show-home on the new housing estate.[39] They are a showcase legal code for the particular historical time and geographical place in which God's "show-home" people, Israel, found themselves. Our lives and communities should have some of the same distinctive qualities that marked out God's people back then, but in other respects our lives and communities will differ significantly. The difficulty for us is distinguishing which laws are still applicable today, and which are not.

Jesus' words on the Sermon on the Mount often confuse us further. Some laws he seems to affirm, others he seems at first glance to contradict, and although he seems to be bringing new teaching, he also states that he has come to fulfil, not abolish, the law, adding, "I tell you the truth, until heaven and earth disappear, not the smallest letter, not the least stroke of a pen, will by any means disappear from the Law until everything is accomplished."[40]

This last statement is foundational for understanding Jesus' life, death and resurrection as the once-in-history worked example or "show home" of perfect law-keeping, as the Israelites failed to live up to God's standards. Jesus simultaneously underlined the importance of the law and yet also he transcended the law, ultimately demonstrating that relationship with God is far more than just keeping rules.

I once had to drive from one side of Amsterdam to the other.

---

39  See Wright, C., 1984, *Living as the People of God: the relevance of Old Testament Ethics*, IVP, for a fuller exploration of these ideas.
40  Matthew 5:17–19.

Fortunately I had a SatNav that knew precisely where the canals and roads were between where I was and where I wanted to be. Unfortunately someone in the town planning office had recently redesigned the city, adding one-way systems, closing bridges, assigning pedestrian-only zones and creating bicycle lanes. I felt like throwing the SatNav into a canal as it barked at me to turn left where I couldn't possibly turn left, but I still relied on it for basic information about where I was in relation to where I was going. Fortunately I also had a friend with me who knew the road changes and could guide me across the city. It is our friend Jesus who helps us to navigate the Old Testament laws because he not only affirms their eternal validity and fulfils their stipulations but also points out which parts are still relevant for our lives.

A rough rule of thumb when it comes to distinguishing between the different laws is to put them into three categories – the ceremonial, the civil and the moral law – and see how Jesus deals with each one.

## The ceremonial law

The ceremonial law relates to the rules of corporate worship that God set for his people, particularly those associated with the Temple, the priesthood and the sacrificial system. These laws help us to understand the New Testament's teaching of Jesus himself as our temple and our sacrifice, and show that therefore we no longer need to follow them.

## The civil law

The civil aspects of the law have to do with the running of the nation of Israel as a holy, separated people, deliberately distinct from those around to act as a conduit of blessing to the other nations. These laws help us understand the New Testament's teaching that Jesus is the fulfilment of all that the nation of Israel was called to do, and he is the Holy One through whom all the nations will be blessed, and so now there is no longer Jew or Gentile[41] in God's plans for his people. In Acts we are clearly told that these laws have been annulled.[42]

## The moral law

The moral aspects of the law are not annulled in the New Testament. On the contrary, Jesus teaches us in the Sermon on the Mount that God

---

41 Colossians 3:11.
42 Acts 10:9–15. See also Mark 7:19.

requires that we keep the spirit and the letter of these laws, before the morally perfect God. For example, he says, "You have heard that it was said, 'Do not commit adultery.' But I tell you that anyone who looks at a woman lustfully has already committed adultery with her in his heart."[43] Jesus' words show us that none of us are able to keep either the spirit or the letter of the law and so we come to recognize that we need him, his perfect law-keeping and his death in our place more than we knew.

In practice the laws don't always fit neatly into each category. For example, the commandment to keep the Sabbath day holy seems to have ceremonial and civil dimensions to it, as well as moral aspects given in the reasons why this law was so important. Daniel Hayes also points out: "The Old Testament itself gives no hint of any such distinctions. For example 'love your neighbor as yourself' (Lev. 19:18) is followed in the very next verse by the law 'do not wear clothing woven of two kinds of material' (19:19)."[44] Bearing this in mind, this framework can still be a useful quick guide when we are reading the books of the law.

When Jesus said he had come to fulfil the law, he was not exaggerating. He not only fulfilled the letter of the law by living a morally perfect life, he also fulfilled the spirit of the law by showing how God's values worked out in practice. Moreover, he also fulfilled the purpose of the law by becoming all that the law was meant to achieve – the means by which God's people could live consistently with the grace they had received from the God who had rescued them from slavery. Jesus is our new, upgraded "show-home": he is the one who now models for us a life lived God's way.

---

43   Matthew 5:27–28.
44   Hayes, J. D., "Applying the Law today", *Bibliotheca Sacra*, Vol. 158:629, 2001, p. 23.

**TRAVEL JOURNAL: Leviticus 19**

1. Read Leviticus 19, and list the laws you find. Try to categorize them under the headings of ceremonial, civil, and moral.

2. How do the obsolete ceremonial laws help us understand Jesus as our perfect sacrifice?

3. How do the obsolete civil laws help us understand God's heart for the nations?

4. How do the ongoing moral laws help us to live a life pleasing to God in light of his grace to us?

# Day 4: **No entry**

It was a hot day and I was running late *and* I was lost – not a great combination. In a sweaty, stressed and rather disjointed way I managed to ask a security guard for directions. His reply was less than helpful: "Sorry, mate, you can't get there from here." Perhaps it was when he saw the colour drain from my face, or my jaw drop to the pavement that he realized the incongruity of his remark. He clarified things slightly, explaining that if I could just relocate myself to the other side of the campus, I would easily find the meeting I was late for. I gave him that look that meant "And do you happen to have a teleportation device up your sleeve?" before I sprinted off to find a more helpful guide.

Life would be so much easier if we didn't have to bother with routes! But when we want to get to know God, his will and his future, we have to start somewhere. Finite, mortal, sinful humans like us need an incredible amount of help to get to know the infinite, immortal and holy Lord of heaven. God does not ask us to teleport ourselves through some blind leap of faith to a position where we sit perfectly at his feet or walk faultlessly in his will. God knows he needs to start where we are and reveals himself to us little by little, as that is what we can handle.

I thought I had chemistry nailed when I was nine years old. I had read an encyclopedia article that cleverly explained that the atoms were to be understood as a set of unbreakable marbles that form the building blocks of everything we see around us. Secondary school added to my understanding by telling me it was better to think of atoms like a Christmas pudding with electrons instead of raisins. Then A-level chemistry came along – atoms were now like planets, with electron moons orbiting them. Finally at university atoms became electromagnetic fields wrapping around a nucleus. I certainly couldn't have handled that aged nine. So was I wrong back then with my marble theory? No. That was the only model my primary school brain could handle, and it served to help me as my teachers wisely built up the concepts that would give me the fuller picture later on.

God in his wisdom took his people on a similar learning journey. He led his people from ignorance to knowledge, drip-feeding them concepts and models over the centuries so that they could be ready for the fullness of truth about God that was revealed in Jesus.

Many people feel that the God of the New Testament contradicts the God of the Old Testament, often quoting the famous "eye for an eye" passage as an example. However, understanding this in terms of God progressively revealing his will and his character through the history of his people can help us to see that these apparent contradictions are actually complementary learning tools. Let's take a closer look at that passage to see how this works:

> *If anyone takes the life of a human being, he must be put to death. Anyone who takes the life of someone's animal must make restitution – life for life. If anyone injures his neighbour, whatever he has done must be done to him: fracture for fracture, eye for eye, tooth for tooth. As he has injured the other, so he is to be injured. Whoever kills an animal must make restitution, but whoever kills a man must be put to death. You are to have the same law for the alien and the native-born. I am the LORD your God.*[45]

To our contemporary world these laws might feel very basic, almost barbaric. The problem is that we compare the Bible passages with our contemporary ethical systems (which have been built on Christian moral assumptions) rather than with how they related to the world of their day. Two perspectives may help us as we handle this difficult-to-swallow moral code. Firstly, if we compare Israel's laws with those of other nations at the time, we notice significant differences. For example, here is an excerpt from the *Laws of Enshunna*, a legal code from 1800 BC:

> *If a free man has no claim against another free man, but seizes the other free man's slave girl, detains the one seized in his house and causes her death, he must give two slave girls to the owner of the slave girl as a compensation. If he has no claim against him but seized the wife or child of an upper class person and causes death, it is a capital crime.*[46]

The laws of Israel were very different because they treated everyone

---

45  Leviticus 24:17–22.
46  Fee, G. D. & Stuart, D., 1982, *How to Read the Bible for all its Worth*, Zondervan, p. 143, quoting Pritchard, J. B. (ed.), 1969, *Ancient Near Eastern Texts Relating to the Old Testament*, third edition, Princetown University Press, p. 162. Reproduced with permission.

equally; no matter who the victim or the perpetrator was, the penalty was the same. Life was not given a monetary value because that would favour the rich and discriminate against the poor.

Secondly, we see that the laws of Israel, instead of escalating violence, radically limited it. Imagine you lived in ancient times and accidentally knocked out some rich landowner's son's tooth. The lack of effective dentists meant you had scarred someone for life and the landowner was likely to be furious at you for defacing his son's precious smile. Without any law, you should brace yourself for the inevitable fact that he would hunt you down on his mission to extract some evil revenge! But no matter how angry or powerful he was, he could not take vengeance into his own hands. A little bit of dental arithmetic would show that the maximum punishment you could expect from the court was the very fair removal of your own tooth, your whole tooth, and nothing but your tooth!

Although this law was fair and foundational to a non-violent society, it was not the end of the story. It was a true but ultimately limited model preparing God's people for the next stage of his revelation of his character, when Jesus says: "You have heard that it was said, 'Eye for eye, and tooth for tooth.' But I tell you, do not resist an evil person. If someone strikes you on the right cheek, turn to him the other also."[47] This is not a contradiction, but rather a continuation with an additional requirement. Whereas previously punishment was limited, now that we know Jesus, we are shown that forgiveness is even better.

Entry-level understanding of living God's way in a fallen world was to grasp that certain requirements were to be met. The law highlighted God's absolute holiness, and reflected his values as summarized by Jesus: "'Love the Lord your God with all your heart and with all your soul and with all your mind.' This is the first and greatest commandment. And the second is like it: 'Love your neighbour as yourself.' All the Law and the Prophets hang on these two commandments."[48] Generations of failure to meet God's standards were supposed to result in that feeling I had from talking to the security guard – a desperate sense of inability to get there from here – to get to God from a fallen world. But God did have something up his

---

47  Matthew 5:38–39.
48  Matthew 22:37–40.

sleeve – a plan to remove the "No Entry" sign and send his own Son to fulfil all the requirements of the law [49] and then take the condemnation that should be ours for failing to live up to the law's standards. Jesus died to be the way to God so that we can get to God from here.

**TRAVEL JOURNAL: Leviticus 25**

1. What clues do you see in this passage that God is beginning to teach his people the key aspects of his character?

2. How is the trajectory of these themes continued through the Bible?

3. Many people think that God was strict in the Old Testament and then lightened up in the New Testament. How does Jesus show in Matthew 5 that the laws are actually increased in their intensity, their scope and their application?

4. If this trajectory is continued beyond Bible times, then the Bible teaching has laid ticking time-bombs under sinful structures and unjust systems – such as the modern-day slave trade or nuclear warfare, for example. How should the church work out how to apply the principles of God's laws for our world today?

---

49  Matthew 5:17–19.

# Day 5: **Concept cars**

The screams were getting louder. They were bloodcurdling screams: eerie, high-pitched, desperate squeals of torture and murder coming from the road behind our apartment. On one side of the road the shoppers were continuing their small-talk as they bought fresh vegetables by the kilo, apparently oblivious to the carnage behind them. Then I watched as they crossed over and paid for a leg of the poor sheep that had just been carved up, carefully avoiding stepping in the sticky stream of blood that made its way through the dirt and down the road.

This scene of animal sacrifice, common in many Muslim countries around the world, made me feel physically sick the first time I witnessed it. It made me see the Old Testament in a new light, and it raised several questions: Why would God advocate blood sacrifices in the law that involved the slaughter of helpless, peaceful, domestic animals? Why would he want the stench and messy entrails and bloodcurdling noise polluting his holy temple?

There is an incredible amount of space given over in the Old Testament to the instructions regarding both animal sacrifice and the details for constructing the tabernacle (or tent of meeting). These are not wasted words. A good rule of Bible reading is to pay close attention to the subject the author devotes a lot of material to. For example, the gospel writers spend far more time on the last week of Jesus' life than any other week in his life. So what is the significance of these swathes of Scripture describing the carnage that was Israel's worship?

### Prototype

I love taking the kids to motor shows and looking at the concept cars. I love the gleaming colours and the strange designs. These machines, dripping with technologies that do not yet exist, may well be what my kids will be driving after I'm dead and gone. Most of these prototypes don't actually work. Often they don't even have engines in them – they are purely a glimpse of the future. The same is true of the sacrifice system in the Old Testament – it is a prototype with no power in it, as we are told in Hebrews: "The law is only a shadow of the good things that are coming – not the realities themselves. For this reason it can never, by the same sacrifices repeated endlessly year after year, make perfect those who draw near to worship."[50] Christianity is not just an alternative religious option for those of us who are squeamish about butchering lambs. The sacrifices were necessary as a prototype pointing forward to the future when Jesus offered himself as a sacrifice for the forgiveness of our sins. Understanding the laws helps us to appreciate the suffering Jesus went through for us on the cross.

## Blueprint

As we read the description of the sacrifices we have an insight into why sacrifice was necessary, how sacrifices work, and what Jesus' life, death and resurrection actually accomplished. Like a blueprint, the description contains far more detail than meets the eye when you look at the finished article. Even a child's toy requires a meticulous blueprint for its design, but looking at one in a shop window, you might never guess. We usually skim over these chapters, wondering why we should care about the dimensions of what appears to be a glorified gazebo, especially when we have just finished reading the first half of Exodus featuring a dramatic victory over an ancient superpower. But the fact that we are only given one chapter for the Passover, one for the destruction of the Egyptian army and then six chapters for the tabernacle shows us how significant it was to Judaism. But the blueprint we are given is for more than just a tent – it is for a visual and experiential learning tool to help God's people to understand how God must be approached. These laws point to God's holiness and the incredible privilege we have in approaching God in prayer as our heavenly Father.

## Security system

The layers of security around a nuclear reactor are a complex system of locked doors, identity checks, air locks, washing procedures and clearance protocols. They are there to protect us from the raw power of the reactor core and from the fatal consequences of human error. So too God makes it clear that we need protection from his presence and from the fatal consequences of human sin. Approaching the centre of the tabernacle involved animal sacrifice, cleansing and offerings.[51] One particularly strong visual aid was the thick curtain that separated the rest of the tabernacle from the Holy of Holies, where the Ark of the Covenant was placed – a

---

50  Hebrews 10:1.
51  For an interesting exploration of the significance of the tabernacle, see Gooding, D., 1989, *An Unshakeable Kingdom*, IVP.

space inaccessible even to the priests. Only one designated cleric, the high priest, could go into the Holy of Holies and only on one day of the year, the Day of Atonement. Entering the presence of a holy God was no smash-and-grab affair – there was a very deliberate and solemn process to navigate the holy obstacle course into the presence of God.

When Jesus died on the cross, Matthew tells us the curtain in the Temple was ripped in two from top to bottom, allowing public, open access to what had previously been almost totally inaccessible. No more sacrifices needed, no more priests, no more security checks. The more we understand the impossible standards of the law, the exacting blueprint of the law, and the meticulous security system of the law, the more we will appreciate what Jesus has done for us. And the more we appreciate that, the more our lives will be marked in every aspect by genuine, grateful worship.

### TRAVEL JOURNAL: Leviticus 16

1. Imagine you were to re-enact the Day of Atonement next Sunday. Make a plan of action, with a rough budget, a schedule and a risk assessment. How do you feel about doing this? How do you imagine people will react?
2. How does this exercise help us to understand God's holiness?
3. How does this exercise help us to appreciate what Jesus has done for us?
4. In light of this, read Romans 12:1–2 and Hebrews 10:19–25. What insights do you now have into these passages? What practical difference do the authors suggest this should make to our day-to-day lives?

## Small Group Study 2
# Living distinctively with the law

Imagine two teenagers were to move into your home for a month. What ground rules would you set at the beginning of the month? What are the unspoken rules they would discover during the course of their stay?

Last week we looked at the trouble God's people got themselves into because "everyone did as they saw fit". This week we saw that God's law was supposed to help his people: "God is not like a harsh headmaster laying down the ground rules on the first day of school. He is more like the kind lifeguard who has just rescued a drowning man and is now telling him to kick off his shoes, don't thrash about, and don't panic" (Week 2, Day 1, page 43).

Debate the following viewpoint by dividing into two groups and building a biblical case for and against this argument. What conclusions can you reach?

> *None of the Old Testament laws have any significance for believers today. Reading the law will only confuse you, as it contradicts the rest of the Bible. Better to ignore those parts of the Bible totally, and just focus on the New Testament.*

What is your reaction to the following laws recorded in the Bible?

⊕ Do not mate different types of animals.[52]

⊕ Do not hold back the wages of a hired worker overnight.[53]

⊕ Do not eat meat with blood in it.[54]

⊕ Do not tattoo yourself.[55]

No reasons are given for these laws, but why do you think they were included? In your two groups build a case for or against each law applying today.

---

52  Leviticus 19:19.
53  Leviticus 19:13.
54  Leviticus 19:26.
55  Leviticus 19:28.

Discuss these dilemmas and then look up the references. How could the examples of God's standards help us form priorities and principles?

| | |
|---|---|
| How should a legal system determine whether rape or embezzlement should receive a longer prison sentence? | Deuteronomy 22:23–36<br>Deuteronomy 25:13–16 |
| A Christian businesswoman wants to find a way to use her company to offer empowering help to the poor in her city. What could she do? | Leviticus 19:9–10 |
| Mary cannot decide if it is worth paying extra for free-range eggs. Does God really care about whether or not chickens are kept in cages, or should she be prudent with her money? | Deuteronomy 25:4 |
| Every European cow is subsidized by over $2.50 a day, which is more than 75 per cent of what Africans have to live on.[56] | Leviticus 25:4 |
| A refugee settlement centre has been set up near your church. What is the church's responsibility to refugee people? | Leviticus 19:34 |

God's people were supposed to be distinctive in what they ate and how they dressed, in their treatment of animals and conduct toward immigrants, in their worship and in their work ethic, in their courts and on their battlefields. Every part of their lives was lived distinctively for God. What should that mean for us? Think of some practical examples of how to live distinctively during the next twenty-four hours.

---

56   Williams, J., 2004, *50 Facts That Should Change the World*, Icon Books, p. 47.

# Week 3: Living poetically

*The psalms and their application to life*

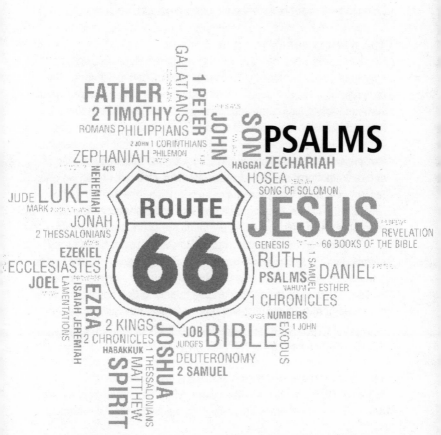

# Day 1: **Playlist**

Thirty years later, and still every time I vacuum the house, I can't help singing the refrain of a TV commercial for "Shake n' Vac" – a product that involved sprinkling a powder onto the floor before vacuuming to ostensibly eradicate foul smells. Somehow this jingle has wormed its way into my head and, like those annoying carpet odours, there's very little I can do to remove it.

Thankfully it's not just the wily advertisers who know the power of a good tune coupled with some catchy words. God in his wisdom inspired 150 strange songs to sit geographically and emotionally at the centre of our Bibles. This week we will look at the book of Psalms, a part of the Old Testament that seems to be particularly treasured by Christians worldwide. It is not hard to see why they have such popular appeal:

## The psalms speak to us and for us

Are the psalms a part of God's word to us, or our words to God? The answer is strangely both. As the psalms are included in Scripture, they form part of God's unique, powerful and utterly truthful, revealed word. Through Psalms, God commands us to praise him, inspires us to worship him and paints vivid pictures of what he is like and what he has done. But as we read the psalms we are also given words that help us express that praise and worship and wonder back to God in a whole myriad of different emotional states and situations. When we talk to God we often run out of words to say; sometimes our situation is so difficult that we cannot think of how to bring it before God, and our prayer life seems so impoverished that borrowing the language of the psalms can jump-start us back into the channels of communication. The psalms give us permission to pray liturgically using words God has given us. The psalms also give us permission to pray freestyle: they record extremely honest prayers, allowing us to feel comfortable to pray to God openly, whatever our mood or tone or circumstance. I often benefit from alternating between the two, allowing the structure of a psalm to fuel the way I express my own feelings and to help me sense God's voice.

## The psalms are both public and private songs

Other people's expectations often shape what we say and how we say it. This is true whether we are talking to friends at a funeral, talking to our children in the supermarket, or talking with God in a prayer meeting. Public expectations of public praying can hinder us from being open and honest, but even our private prayers are often terse and dispassionate, as though we are bound by some invisible regulation book. The psalms challenge us with their raw, intense honesty, often saying things in a public hymn-book that we would struggle to say even in the privacy of our bedrooms. David, the king of Israel, is not ashamed to publicly confess his weaknesses and run to God for help. He models humility and the integrity that proves that his internal world is seamlessly related to his public life.

## The psalms speak both of hope and despair

I struggle with people who have no struggles. Our local traffic warden, for one, always appears to be extremely satisfied with her life to the point of smugness, getting her daily kicks by doling out suffering she will never experience to unsuspecting car owners who have inadvertently parked over the line or over the limit. The psalms don't allow Christians to imagine that the life of faith will be one of continued smug triumph and victory, while all around us suffer. All sorts of struggles, emotions and tragedies are legitimized here in the centre of our Bibles, making the book of Psalms particularly precious to Christians who understand from experience that the life of faith involves doubt, anxiety, temptation and persecution as well as joy, hope and love.

To our shame, my wife and I often communicate by email as we inform each other when the MOT is due or why the school was trying to get hold of us or how the printer has stopped working – again. Our busy world seems far removed from when we had the time and inclination to read *Romeo and Juliet* while gazing into each other's eyes! Sometimes the way we talk with God heads in the same direction as we reel off names of acquaintances in the local hospital for him to heal, or events in the church's calendar for him to bless. Reading the psalms like a date night with your spouse or a regular work-place team meeting, is a way of spending quality time with God. It protects us from the build-up of silence, stonewalling and stand-off, and reminds us how good it is to listen and be listened to by the one who really cares. By allowing the strange songs of the psalms to shape our prayer life, we can transform our prayer times from a shopping list of requests to a playlist of music. God now sets the tone, the rhythm and the pace of our prayer life, not us. As you go about your daily life, whether it is vacuuming the house or paying your parking fines, allow God's songs to be the spiritual soundtrack to your prayers.

## TRAVEL JOURNAL: Psalm 27

1. Use this psalm as a conversation starter between you and God.
2. Note down what this psalm is allowing you to express to God. How is David's example of intimacy and resolve challenging to you?
3. What do you sense God is saying to you through this psalm? What aspects of God's character stand out?
4. Invent a catchy jingle using some of the words of this psalm. Sing them over and over until they have wormed their way into your head. Take note every time they pop up during the rest of the day.

# Day 2: **Repeat mode**

Sometimes singing Christian worship songs drives me insane. Of course, I dare not show it, but inwardly I am begging the band not to do any more woo-hoos, yeah-yeahs or hallelujahs. I have been to some Christian conferences where I am vigorously clapping out of sheer relief that the song has finally come to an end, when the leader makes us start again right from the beginning! Maybe she thought I was clapping for an encore. So we begin again and the more I look at the lyrics the less they seem to make sense, especially given what I am facing in my own life. Cheap rhymes, trite clichés, endless repetition and endless repetition, not to mention endless repetition, drive me insane.

Before you think I am the sort of man who hates singing, you should know that during the global coronavirus pandemic, my daughter and I helped keep each other sane by writing worship songs together and then singing them out as loudly as our voices could manage. But compare the song list of any given church in a Sunday service and you'll struggle to find anything like the rich diversity of lyrics contained in Israel's hymn-book – Psalms.

There are psalms of lament, of thanksgiving, of confidence, and of remembrance. There are wisdom psalms and kingship psalms; psalms for a coronation and psalms for a pilgrimage, as well as hymns of praise. Some psalms do in fact contain repetition, such as the responsive Psalm 118 that repeats the phrase, "his love endures forever". We can imagine this was very helpful in non-literate cultures, but despite the repetition, nobody can accuse this psalm of being shallow. Between the repeated declarations of God's eternal love there is a powerful retelling of the whole story of Israel's history.

The book of Psalms was not only Israel's hymn-book, it was also Israel's history book and theology book. The people of God were encouraged to sing out their beliefs and their memories and their emotions, setting a high standard for depth in corporate sung worship. The psalms model simultaneously engaging emotionally with doctrine and engaging doctrinally with emotion. I would love to see more of this combination in our own sung worship.

## It's about what we sing

Often it is what we sing, more than what we preach, that shapes what we believe. This is partly because rhyme and repetition aid the memory, and partly because singing can be seen as more important or more enjoyable or more participative than hearing preaching. It is partly due to the fact that we sing songs written by the world-class masters of their trade whereas we hear sermons from the averagely competent preacher. It is also partly due to the power of music that touches our emotions and underlines the lyrics we sing. Whatever the reason, the fact remains that when most people leave a church meeting or conference, they can remember the songs they sang far more easily than the challenge laid out by the preacher. This is why it is so important that the lyrics are as strong in truth and sentiment as the music is strong in tempo and timbre.

## It's about who we sing with

I once had a friend who was training to be a tank commander. His training was rigorous – physical workouts, lessons in strategy, technical drills, weaponry know-how, and that was before he even got into the tank. He worked hard, knowing this was no academic exercise. Shortly after his training he was sent to the front line of the action. But while training, the little time he had to relax with his peers was often spent singing, which did more for team building and morale than any military exercise could achieve. It instilled in them a connection and a passion, and when things got tough those songs gave them a welcome distraction, a shared language and a means of expressing their emotions. As we sing together in community, it should be less about creating a bridge from band to congregation, and more about creating a bond between each other that will outlast the music.

## It's about when we sing

If I find it hard to sing in church at the best of times, there is very little hope when times are tough. But the tank commander's team and the book of Psalms agree that it is when things get tough that singing is a lifeline. The problem is that we are so used to our modern worship songs being upbeat, that we do not yet have a playlist in our minds and memories of lyrics that are useful in tough times. Recently there have been a few good songs written to redress the balance, but while these are working their way into our heads and our hearts, into our doctrine and our daily life, perhaps we need to go back to the psalms. They are a gift to us in good times and bad times alike, and we can give them as a gift to others as words of praise in their times of celebration and words of comfort in their times of distress.

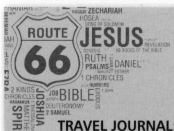

**TRAVEL JOURNAL: Psalm 86**

1. What sort of psalm is this – lament, thanksgiving, confidence, remembrance, wisdom, kingship, coronation, pilgrimage or hymn?

2. How does this psalm combine doctrine and emotion, prayer and praise, supplication and declaration?

3. This intensely personal prayer is meant to be sung publicly. How would the author be helped by singing this song with others? How would other people be helped?

4. Try to describe the situation David is in, according to the clues in this psalm. How could his words help you in difficult circumstances?

# Day 3: **Soundproof**

A moving car is like a choir with several voices working together in harmony. The drone of the engines and the hum of the tyres and the whisper of the air conditioning blend in with the music coming out of the speakers, resulting in a totally immersive driving symphony. But occasionally a dissonant note will sound that will put the driver into hyper-alert mode. I don't know much about mechanics but I know that if I hear certain sounds, I pull over immediately. That *ker-thump, hiss, bleep* or *clank* is the only voice the car has to tell me that something is seriously wrong.

By learning to recognize the voices in the psalms, we will begin to understand better what is normal and healthy in our own emotional environment and prayer life, and what is not. The psalms help us to express all sorts of emotions, and they also help us to relate those emotions to the big story of the Bible.

## Discover the voice – the emotion

David wrote about half of the psalms; others were written by Asaph, Solomon and Moses; and a lot were written by that prolific and elusive author, "Anonymous"! Although we know quite a bit about the ups and downs of David's, Solomon's and Moses' lives, we come to most of the psalms with very little context. We can't read the body language of the psalmist or make a judgment based on whether the music is in a major or minor key – all we have to go on are the voices. It is not hard to hear in those voices the underlying raw emotions of the psalmists, which can range from pain, powerlessness and panic to praise, passion and peace. The voices of the psalms give us a voice to legitimately express these emotions to God.

## Discover the voice – the context

We can immediately empathize with many of the emotions that the psalmists express. However, these cries of the heart are also filled with references to events from Israel's history and to Israel's law. The psalms do more than provide emotional comfort – they can be the key to unlock the less accessible parts of the Bible and introduce us to the voices of the narrative literature and the law. For example, when the psalmist wants to remind himself and the people of Israel of God's faithfulness, he reminds them of God's dealing with his people through the ages.[57] He recognizes that this particular aspect of God's character has been true throughout history and recalls significant occasions from a national, global, or even cosmic perspective.

## Discover the voice – the prophetic

Psalms is quoted more times in the New Testament than any other Old Testament book.[58] The psalms are often treated as a prophetic voice, as particular psalms point to Jesus – his life, death and resurrection – a facet we will come back to on Day 5 of this week. For now, it is worth noting that right in the centre of the Bible we have a hymn-book that points both backwards and forwards in history and introduces us to voices from the whole of Scripture.

## Discover the voice – the dissonance

Old Testament scholar Walter Brueggemann[59] argues that the psalms are a particular gift to God's people wrestling with the disparity between our expectations of the life of faith and the harsh realities of life in a broken world. As we get older we tend to find that the neat little systems we have constructed to help us understand God and his universe don't quite work out as we had hoped. Our belief in the power of forgiveness, for example, might be pushed beyond all limits if our marriage breaks down, or if we experience bullying in the workplace. Our confidence in God for the future may be shaken to the core if a close friend is diagnosed with a terminal condition, or if our pastor admits to gross misconduct. The psalms are realistic rather than idealistic, dealing with the messiness and complexity of real-life faith. For this reason, sometimes we hear more than one voice in each psalm, as there is a clash of emotions between faith and doubt, despair and hope, resignation and determination. But this dissonance doesn't mean we need to pull over onto the hard shoulder and give up moving forward with God. This is a healthy dissonance that encourages an authentic, open faith rather than a simplistic system, and allows us to keep going when we hear those dissonant voices in our heads.

---

57  Psalm 106 is a good example of this.
58  Longman, T., 1988, *How to Read the Psalms*, IVP, p. 65.
59  See Brueggemann, W., 2007, *Praying the Psalms: Engaging Scripture and the Life of the Spirit*, Cascade Books, pp. 1–15.

## Discover the voice – the intimacy

The voices of the psalms help us to find our own voice. They express the messiness of our emotions and encourage us to hold on to our faith, whatever our circumstances throw at us. They also force us to reconsider the reality of our worship, challenging us whether we are content with anodyne routines or if there is a genuine heartfelt relationship with God that is able to face difficult issues head on. The psalms balance the awe of God's majesty with a willingness to disclose to God things we might well be embarrassed to say to anyone but our closest friends, demonstrating an intimacy with God that is unrivalled in any religious text I have come across.

As a Christian student I thought it was my duty to "exhibit the joy of the Lord", as though my grin and my buoyant mood and my cheery voice was a visible evangelistic tract, or a sign of spiritual maturity. I even tried falling asleep smiling so I would develop laughter lines that would give the impression of happiness, however I was feeling inside. But my housemates soon tired of my cheerfulness, especially when they had just woken up, when they had suffered a boring lecture, when their boyfriends had dumped them, when they had no money for food or when they missed home. I was wrong – it was not emotional joviality that I needed to exhibit, but emotional literacy as taught in Psalms – the ability to express and deal with all sorts of emotions in myself and in others.

## TRAVEL JOURNAL: Psalm 22

1. Take two highlighter pens and try to find the two voices in this psalm, one which exhibits pain and isolation from God, and the other which speaks of hope, faith and trust. Do you think there are two people having a conversation or one person wrestling with conflicting feelings?

2. How does the fact that this wrestle of faith is included in the inspired canon of Scripture encourage you as a believer?

3. After reading this psalm, how could you go about helping a Christian friend who says: "I am not sure I believe any more. We prayed every day for her cancer to be healed, but she died anyway. How can I keep believing when this has happened? God just feels so distant."

4. Find the historical (references to Israel's history) and prophetic (references to Jesus) verses in this psalm. How does knowing that Jesus himself quotes this psalm in his darkest hour (Matthew 27:46) help us develop intimacy with God?

# Day 4: **Speed-bumps**

As Mr Keating dictates from his textbook, the students take copious notes and replicate the diagrams in silence. Then, to their complete astonishment, he calmly asks them to rip out the pages on analyzing poetry and discard them completely. The 1989 film *Dead Poets Society* had a huge impact on my generation and many of my peers ended up as teachers as a result. Keating kindled in the students a passion for poetry based on experience and emotions, not on dissecting and analyzing the literary structures. This is equally true for the psalms; they are not meant to be held at arm's length, taken apart and admired for their literary qualities. They are to be lived, prayed, digested, and sung.

Appreciating the beauty of the form of the psalms, understanding how they were written and how they function, should not be an excuse to disengage from the experience of the psalms; rather, it should enhance our love for them. Today we are going to look at the dominant devices the psalmists use to convey what is on their heart.

If God had inspired the psalms to rhyme or rhythmically scan, then the translators may still have been hard at work to find equivalents in the English language! But God in his wisdom inspired the psalms (as well as some of the prophetic writings) to be predominantly written using a simple device called parallelism where it is not couplets of words, but couplets of ideas that rhyme. This device not only showcases the creativity and skill of the writers, but is also used to underline or emphasize the themes of the psalm.

There are many different types of parallelism in the psalms,[60] and being aware of them can help us to hear God's voice more accurately. Here are just three examples of how parallelisms can draw us into the poetry and help us to memorize it and live it.

---

60  See Longman, T., 1998, *How to Read the Psalms*, IVP, pp. 95–110.

## Stick-shift parallels

Here is an example from Psalm 2 where the parallel ideas function like a car moving through the gears to get up to speed:

> *Why do the nations conspire*
> *and the peoples plot in vain?*
> *The kings of the earth take their stand*
> *and the rulers gather together*
> *against the LORD*
> *and against his Anointed One.*

The ideas in the first line are echoed in the second line: nations and peoples, conspiring and plotting. Similarly in the next verse, we see parallels between kings and rulers as they rise up and band together. But often in a parallelism of this sort we can see an increase in intensity in the second line. In our example the addition of the words "in vain" and "against the LORD" points to the main thrust of the psalm: even though the psalmist was living in a time of international political uncertainty, he knew that God was ultimately in control.

## Crossroads parallels (contrast or antithetical)

> *For the LORD watches over the way of the righteous,*
> *but the way of the wicked will perish.*[61]

Here, the second type of parallelism highlights a contrast by placing two opposing ideas side by side. This verse clearly shows a contrast between the way of the righteous and the way of the wicked, which is a key theme in Psalm 1. When you notice this sort of parallelism, take time to check which side of the parallelism you are on. They are often designed

---

61 Psalm 1:6.

as deliberate crossroads to force us to consider whether we are on the right path or not.

## Scenic parallels (thematic or metaphorical)

*As the deer pants for streams of water,*
*so my soul pants for you, O God.*[62]

In this type of parallelism a metaphor is introduced in the first line which is then explained in the second line. When you notice this kind of parallelism, stop and try to picture the image the psalmist is trying to place in your head, as it is there to add richness to your prayer life. By lodging images in our minds, we begin to draw associations with them, aiding the memory and inspiring our own creativity in prayer and worship.

I spend a lot of time scanning articles on the Internet, speed-reading books to review, or trawling through emails on my phone. As a result I find that I now habitually read at a fast pace, extracting the vital facts and discarding the rest. Poetry can't be read like that, and so the parallelisms act as a kind of mental speed-bump, deliberately slowing me down so I can concentrate on God's word, and make time to hear God's voice. In the frenetic pace of modern life the psalms themselves also act as speed bumps, reminding us to reflect on what is going on around us, to reflect on our own emotional health and to reflect on what God is saying to us and through us.

---

62  Psalm 42:1.

**TRAVEL JOURNAL: Psalm 2**

1. Read Psalm 2 through at your normal speed. Then close your Bible and see what you can remember. What is it about?

2. Read Psalm 2 using the parallelisms to slow you down. How many types of parallelism can you find? Close your Bible again – what strikes you differently this time?

3. How do the various parallelisms help us understand how David can remain confident despite international conspiracy against him?

4. This psalm is often quoted with respect to Jesus – see Acts 4:23–31. Knowing that Jesus is the Lord's anointed, the Son of David, the Son of God, how does this psalm reveal a bigger picture of Christ and give you fuel to worship him?

# Day 5: **Getting closer**

In an office in Belfast, a friend of mine made a discovery. It was a doorknob, sculpted into the shape of a lion's head and set at the eye level of an eight-year-old. The beauty of the doorknob became even more significant when he realized that those offices had been converted from an old manse, which had been the family home where C. S. Lewis grew up. Now, whenever I read about Aslan, I imagine Lewis remembering that doorknob.

Lewis has always been one of my heroes. The Narnia series was a highlight of my childhood, and his apologetic writings have heavily influenced my faith. My eldest son even has Lewis for a middle name! One day I hope to visit my friend in his workplace so I can see the doorknob for myself. I have been to Lewis' other home – The Kilns in Oxford – where he spent the last thirty-four years of his life. It was great to see the view from his window and imagine him dreaming up Narnia, and sit in his chair and imagine him reading the background material for his radio broadcasts that would become *Mere Christianity*.[63]

Gazing out of his windows, sitting in his chair and holding a book that Lewis would have read made me feel that he was almost there in the room with me. I had an insight into what his life was like and how his mind was shaped, and I felt like I was getting closer to him. Sometimes when I read the psalms, I feel the same way about my greater hero – Jesus. I have no doubt that Jesus loved and read and sang and prayed the psalms; of all the books in the Bible that he quotes, Psalms is the most frequent. If Jesus was all about the psalms, the psalms are also all about Jesus – they speak for Jesus, of Jesus and to Jesus.

The psalms speak *for Jesus* as they give him words to say in the middle of great joy and great pain. When he enters Jerusalem on a donkey, he is met by a flash mob, as the crowds sing and celebrate and offer their coats for the first-century red-carpet treatment. But when the religious wet-blanket leaders criticize Jesus for the way the children are getting into the spirit of the occasion, Jesus quotes Psalm 8: "from the lips of children and infants you have ordained praise" (Matthew 21:16). Jesus saw the psalm being fulfilled in the joy and

---

63   Lewis, C. S., 1952, *Mere Christianity*, HarperCollins.

jubilation of the buzz of praise around him. At the other extreme, he also expresses the rawness of his pain and isolation on the cross by using words from Psalm 22: "My God, my God, why have you forsaken me?"

The psalms speak *of Jesus* [64] as they are filled with prophecies about his life, death and resurrection. Jesus used the psalms to explain who he was and what would happen to him – for example, on the Emmaus road (Luke 24:44).

The gospel writers also often explained the significance of events in Jesus' life by referring to the psalms.[65]

| Psalm | Gospel reference | Link |
| --- | --- | --- |
| Psalm 2 | Matthew 3:17 | God the Father declares Jesus to be his Son at his baptism. |
| Psalm 22 | Matthew 27:46 | Jesus predicts his rejection and the mocking that will surround his death. |
| Psalm 118 | Luke 20:17 | Jesus explains that he is like the capstone – the foundation of a construction – and that he would be rejected. |
| Psalm 110 | Luke 20:41–44 | Jesus explains that King David called the promised Messiah "Lord", hinting at Jesus' divinity. |
| Psalm 69 | John 15:25 | Jesus explains how the irrational rejection he received was foreseen. |
| Psalm 16; Psalm 110 | Acts 2:25–40 | Peter explains how the psalms predicted the resurrection. |

---

64   See Dillard, R. B. & Longman, T., 1995, *An Introduction to the Old Testament*, IVP, p. 233.

65   The prophetic psalms function in the same way as the other prophetic elements in the Old Testament. They would have first spoken to the original audience offering challenge, hope and encouragement, but when Jesus comes he completes the psalm, showing how his life and actions express the truth of the psalm more fully.

The psalms also speak *to Jesus*. In Hebrews 1 the writer commits blasphemy in the eyes of many Jews by taking words from songs about God the Father and applying them to Jesus. This would have been as shocking to them as changing the words of the old hymn "Praise My Soul the King of Heaven" to "Praise My Soul the Mayor of Cheltenham".

> *But about the Son he says, "Your throne, O God, will last for ever and ever, and righteousness will be the sceptre of your kingdom. You have loved righteousness and hated wickedness; therefore God, your God, has set you above your companions by anointing you with the oil of joy."*[66]

The psalm he quotes is a wedding psalm for a king, but the language is so extravagant there is no way any earthly king will ever measure up to this. The passage can either be understood as extreme hyperbole or divinely inspired prophecy. The writer to the Hebrews understands that, looking back from his post-resurrection standpoint, the psalm points us to the perfections and dimensions of Christ's reign. In a similar way, the Hebrews passage goes on to use the psalmist's words to show that Jesus is not only the King of the world, but also the Creator of the world and the Judge of the world.

Many years ago, and many miles away from the Oxfordshire home we now live in, my wife and I spent a week of sleepless nights on the floor under a table beneath a window in our house. Each evening when darkness fell the skies were filled with the sounds of machine-gunfire, and each morning we would walk streets lined with the casings of the bullets and notice the chips in the walls. As we lay awake playing a grim game of guessing how far away each round of shots could be, we read the psalms together. Sometimes we needed to remember God's sovereignty in the bizarre situation we found ourselves caught up in. Sometimes we wanted to praise God for our well-being. Sometimes we wanted to cry for help and strength. We found that the psalms gave us comfort and courage as we sought God's peace. But, more importantly, just like the strange feeling I got sitting in Lewis's study, knowing that we were using the same words Jesus used when he was in distress, helped us feel closer to him.

---

66  Hebrews 1:8–9; Psalm 45:6–7.

## TRAVEL JOURNAL: Psalm 69

1. Which aspects of Jesus' early life and ministry are prophesied in verses 1–10? (Compare John 15:18–25; 7:1–7; 2:13–17.) How does it help us to know that Jesus faced these struggles?

2. The way Jesus dealt with people who opposed him is supposed to be an example for us (see Romans 15:1–6). How is this psalm a model of a Christlike way of coping with our pain?

3. Read verses 19–28. David is linking his unjust suffering with the pouring out of God's wrath. How is this perfectly fulfilled in Jesus? Compare the passage with Matthew 27:32–50.

4. The hope of verses 30–36 is a stark contrast to the distress of the earlier verses. How do Jesus' life and death bring these things together? How can this help us when we go through difficult times?

# Small Group Study 3
# **Living poetically with the psalms**

The English language has around 3,000 adjectives to describe how we feel. In pairs, how many words can you write down in sixty seconds that could complete the sentence: "I feel…"?

How many of these emotions are expressed in our normal Sunday morning songs at church? Why do you think we find it difficult to talk about our feelings to each other and to God? Which emotions do we find it most difficult to express?

Many Christians have a favourite psalm. Which is yours, why do you love it, and when has it meant most to you? If you haven't got a favourite psalm, what would you look for?

Scan through these psalms – match the psalms with the emotions described. Compare the beginning and end of each psalm to see if or how the psalmist reconciles his emotions.

| Psalm | Emotion |
|-------|---------|
| 18 | I feel guilty |
| 19 | I feel secure |
| 23 | I feel awe |
| 42 | I feel betrayed |
| 51 | I feel content |
| 55 | I feel depressed |
| 64 | I feel relieved |
| 125 | I feel angry |

Not only do the psalms help us to unlock and express our emotions, they also help us to unlock and express the rest of the Bible. By holding our emotions out in one hand, and holding on to the fundamental realities of the world in the other, we can keep our emotional life in balance.

Match the following psalms with the different major events of the Bible:

| Psalm | Key Event |
|-------|-----------|
| 2 | Creation |
| 16 | Law |
| 22 | History |
| 50 | Prophets |
| 74 | Kings |
| 104 | Jesus' death |
| 105 | Jesus' resurrection |
| 82 | Judgment |

The psalms make use of both the history and the future of God's people as fuel for worship. How can we make sure we are drawing on the whole of Scripture to help us worship God more fully?

Write a psalm together as a small group. Encourage each member to write anonymously on a piece of paper, expressing how they are feeling and some words of Scripture that they are holding on to. Collect up the papers and read them out one after another as your prayer time. Here is an example:

*The Lord is my shepherd, but I feel lost.*
*I long for my husband to be healed physically and freed from the worry that is tearing him apart. O Lord, your will be done.*
*I am excited by the prospect of the year ahead. Because your love is better than life, my lips will glorify you.*
*I feel discouraged because of my work situation. I also know that God can do immeasurably more than all I can ask or imagine.*

# Week 4: **Living discerningly**

*The wisdom literature and its application to life*

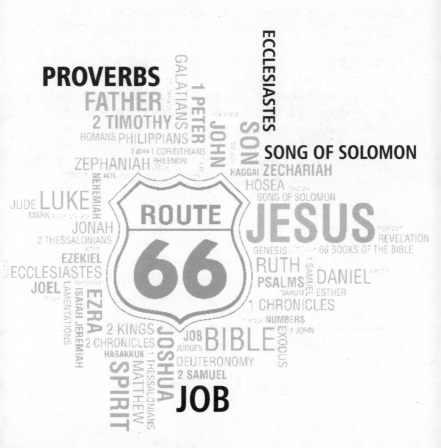

# Day 1: **Crossroads**

Everyone is offering advice these days. As I drive home I hear the words of an obnoxious motoring journalist taunting me as I imagine what life would be like if I had a car that could zoom through speed cameras faster than they could zap me. When I get home, I hear my super keen online fitness coach tell me why I should be working out more. When I sit down for dinner, I wonder what that trendy celebrity chef would say about the smell and tastes that I have concocted. When I go to bed, I wonder what I will get for my birthday – no doubt it will include new books promising to help me make decisions about clothes, diet, food, sleep and everything in between.

In the information age we are drowning in tips and tricks as well as facts and figures. Because there are endless permutations on insurance deals, air-fares and phone contracts, we become dependent on those young experts at the end of a phone line, or on the TV screen to help us make the right decision at every crossroad of our lives. So why is it, with all the wisdom flying around today, that our nations still fall into recession, relationships still break down irreparably and world resources are still so unfairly distributed that half the world is dying of starvation while the other half is dying from obesity?

Perhaps it's time we looked deeper for real wisdom, and started to listen to the Creator's advice[67] on what life is for and how to make the best of it. Life has always been full of choices and in the wisdom literature of the Bible God himself offers us help to navigate the maze of options before us.

Our journey this week through the wisdom literature starts with the "orthodox"[68] wisdom of Proverbs and moves on to what has been termed the "radical" wisdom of Ecclesiastes, Job and the Song of Solomon. The "orthodox" wisdom could be compared to basic driving lessons around nice, quiet roads, while the "radical" wisdom assumes that you have that training in place and offers advanced skills of coping in extreme conditions.

The book of Proverbs at first glance looks like a random collection

---

67   The wisdom literature has a greater emphasis on God as creator than God as redeemer. "With some exceptions, these proverbs do not refer explicitly to God, the history of redemption, or the covenant." Dillard, R. B. & Longman, T., 1995, *An Introduction to the Old Testament*, IVP, p. 243.
68   See Birch, B. C., Brueggemann, W., Fretheim, T. E. & Petersen, D. L. ,1999, *A Theological Introduction to the Old Testament*, Abingdon, pp. 392–393.

of sayings but it roughly divides into three categories. The first nine chapters set the tone: they introduce us to a father who is trying to educate his teenage son in the school of life as an adult. We see that this book is a sincere gift of love and grace, and it reminds us that this part of the Bible is not another list of rules, but is a straight-talking rough guide to life freely given to us by our heavenly Father to equip us for all that lies ahead of us. The next six chapters are all about character and consequences, and the rest of the book is a collection of other wisdom sayings neatly concluding with the description of the perfect woman, who stands in stark contrast to the wayward woman introduced in chapter 1.

Many people want the Bible to be a "How To" guide for life, and are disappointed when they look for advice on how to cope with a pushy car salesman or how to react when they have been overlooked for a rota at church. But the Bible would be an endless book if it had to cover all our dilemmas. Personally, I wish it would tell me what to say to the IT manager when I have broken my fourth phone in six months, or what to do when I run over my own laptop or accidently kill the family pet. (All things I have actually managed to do!) The book of Proverbs may be the best place to start when looking for advice, but we should recognize that the counsel given is in broad categories. For example, wisdom is given regarding relationships, work and financial matters as test cases for how reflection on God's creation can give us the tools to live well for him.

Ultimately all our dilemmas boil down to the overarching theme of Proverbs, as summed up in chapter 9: "The fear of the Lord is the beginning of wisdom, and knowledge of the Holy One is understanding" (verse 10). The most important lesson and the dominant theme of the wisdom literature is that in order to live life well here in creation, we should ensure that we are relating properly to our Creator. This is more than simply remembering God's existence. The writer refers to God as Yahweh – the specific and personal name of the unchanging, holy God who seeks an intimate relationship with each one of us.

The book of Proverbs, with its numerous sayings on an enormous variety of issues, can basically be summarized by the fact that ultimately we have to choose between two ways to live – God's way or our own way. Some of the proverbs state this explicitly, while some use metaphors to imply that at the heart of every choice in life is the question of allegiance.

This theme of whether or not we will give God our allegiance overflows into the rest of the Bible. It is the opening question of the book of Psalms,[69] and the dominant theme of the Sermon on the Mount where Jesus differentiates between the narrow and wide gates, true and false prophets, trees bearing good and bad fruit, true and false discipleship and the wise and foolish builders.[70] It is the question we face daily as we stand at each crossroads and have to choose whether we will dare to live God's way, taking the opportunity to express reverent devotion to Yahweh, or whether we will follow the flow of the crowd.

## TRAVEL JOURNAL: Proverbs 1 – 9

1. Summarize the benefits of wisdom outlined in Proverbs 1:1–6.
2. Fill in this table:

| | What is the dominant metaphor? | What are the consequences of the two options? |
| --- | --- | --- |
| Proverbs 2:5–11, 12–22 | | |
| Proverbs 4:10–19 | | |
| Proverbs 7:10–23; 8:1–12 | | |

3. Are there any complex decisions you are facing?
4. How does each of your options give you the opportunity to express allegiance to God?

---

69  Psalm 1 emphasizes this choice of living for God or following the ways of the wicked, and Psalm 2 encourages nations to make peace with God's Messiah.
70  Matthew 7:13–27.

# Day 2: **Speed-traps**

I promised myself I wasn't going to like it, but I just couldn't help myself. As I watched the film, I was drawn into the story of the American boy who goes to live in China, and gets bullied at school by a group of teenage kung fu experts. The maintenance worker begins to train the lad in self-defence simply by getting him to practise taking off his coat, putting it on the floor and hanging it up over and over again. Once he has mastered his wardrobe dysfunction, this young African American boy is then able, in apparently no time at all, to duck and dive, punch and kick his way to the final of the biggest youth kung fu competition in China! *The Karate Kid*[71] the movie made me cry and cheer as zero turned to hero before my very eyes.

The five-minute training montage is a common device used in movies to show how an amateur can turn into a pro in the time it takes to play just one inspiring song. These Hollywood instant transformations can lead us to expect change more quickly than is reasonably or physically possible. Matthew Syed in his book *Bounce: How Champions are Made*[72] argues that, contrary to popular opinion, success is not based on talent or genetics but is down to sheer hard work and practice. He argues that it takes 10,000 hours of practice to become a world-class champion. He speaks from his personal experience of becoming a number-one-seed table-tennis player. But sadly, even when we put in the hours, we still often only stumble along in "average". Some of us may well have spent 10,000 hours driving a car and yet we are nowhere near Formula 1 standard. In fact sometimes the longer we spend at the wheel, the worse we drive!

Some of us expect to see instant results in our spiritual development, as though we could become wise overnight. Some of us have been disciples for a very long time, but we are still none the wiser. The way that Proverbs deals with this dichotomy is to offer us three apparent contradictions. Being aware of these contradictions should help us as we approach the whole of the wisdom literature.

---

71  *The Karate Kid*, 2010, Colombia Pictures, directed by Harald Zwart – a remake of *The Karate Kid*, 1984, Colombia Pictures.
72  Syed, M., 2010, *Bounce: How Champions are Made*, Fourth Estate.

## Wisdom – a gift or a skill?

> *My son, if you accept my words and store up my commands*
> *within you, turning your ear to wisdom and applying your heart*
> *to understanding, and if you call out for insight and cry aloud for*
> *understanding, and if you look for it as for silver and search for*
> *it as for hidden treasure, then you will understand the fear of the*
> *Lord and find the knowledge of God. For the Lord gives wisdom,*
> *and from his mouth come knowledge and understanding.*[73]

The words and images that the proverbs use to describe the way we
attain wisdom are active and intentional. There is clearly a need to
practise, practise, practise and pray, pray, pray. As we meditate on the
book of Proverbs and apply them to our decisions, then our minds are
trained and moulded into patterns of thinking that overflow into every
area of our lives. Wisdom is clearly portrayed in Scripture as a skill that
takes a lifetime to perfect. However, wisdom is also clearly portrayed
as a free gift from God. However much we learn it, we can't earn it.
Remembering this tension will keep us striving toward wisdom without
allowing us to become proud.

## Wisdom – theory or practice?

A lot of the proverbs seem to offer advice that sounds very reasonable
on paper, but doesn't seem very reliable in practice. For example, one
common theme of the proverbs seems to be that hard work leads to
prosperity,[74] but laziness leads to poverty.[75] At first glance this appears
to be sound business advice. However, the reality is that there are many
honest, hard-working people in poverty through no fault of their own,
and there seem to be many extremely lazy wealthy people. Can it be that
the proverbs are training us to think in false categories?

The general principle of hard work leading to financial stability is
a legitimate one – it is the basis of economies around the world. But
although much of the wisdom literature is descriptive of predictable
consequences, we should beware of turning a *principle* into a *promise*.
The proverbs describe the way things normally work out, but they do not
come with a fail-safe guarantee that they will always work out that way.

---

73  Proverbs 2:1–6.
74  Proverbs 14:23.
75  Proverbs 6:10–11.

The fact that most A-grade students end up becoming homeowners does not mean that working hard at school will guarantee you a six-figure salary. Putting 150 per cent effort in at work on any given day does not mean that the red letters on your doorstep will evaporate into thin air by the time you come home at night.

Secondly, we should beware of turning a *principle* into a *precedent*. The world is not as God intended and sin has infected the world to such a degree that its viral qualities have messed with the normal cause and effect of hard work and just reward. Working hard may well mean prosperity – but not necessarily for the one who works hard. Children may slave away in sweatshops in India turning a tidy profit for British entrepreneurs, but who gets to sit by the pool in designer swimwear at the end of the day?

Thirdly, we should beware of turning a *principle* into a *presumption*. The book of Job clearly short-circuits the simplistic logic that hard work guarantees personal wealth, as we see him stripped of all he owns as a result of some supernatural wager.

## Wisdom – confirms or contradicts?

Even the internal logic of the book of Proverbs guards us against seeing these parts of the Bible too simplistically as "The dummies' guide to wisdom". Proverbs 26:4 says: "Do not answer a fool according to his folly, or you will be like him yourself", while the very next verse exhorts us to do the exact opposite: "Answer a fool according to his folly, or he will be wise in his own eyes." Clearly we cannot use the proverbs as a rigid, mechanistic answer to all life's problems, applying them universally as blanket rules. Some fools need to be treated one way, others need to be treated in the opposite way.

## Karate wisdom?

*The Karate Kid* shows us that practising certain skills over and over will make us generally stronger, faster and more agile in our thinking. But unlike *The Karate Kid*, this will not be accomplished in a week, a month, a year or even a decade. The pursuit of wisdom is supposed to be a lifelong ambition. The proverbs are God's training tool for us to think in a godly way, and as our grasp of them grows we will avoid jumping to simplistic conclusions and will leave room for the exceptions to the rule and the messiness of a broken and fallen world.

### TRAVEL JOURNAL: Proverbs 3

1. How does chapter 3 encourage you to be active in seeking out wisdom, but also cautious about claiming to be wise?

2. Which verses affirm your own experience? Which verses contradict your own experience and how can you reconcile this?

3. How are we to deal with the apparent contradictions in Proverbs 3: "lean not on your own understanding" (verse 5) and "Blessed is the man… who gains understanding" (13); wisdom brings rewards (16) and yet wisdom is a reward in itself (15); God will bless you (18) and God will discipline you (11)?

4. How do these verses, that cover everything from tithing to good neighbourly practice to discipline, help to bring us back to who God is and what he is like?

# Day 3: **Biting-point**

Before his first-ever Sunday school lesson, the teacher was called out to the front of the church to be commissioned into his role. His pastor was very excited and enthusiastically prayed for him, thanking God for his gifts, his gender (all the other Sunday school teachers were women), his willingness to step forward to this vital ministry, and for all the children who he would bless on a Sunday morning. At the end of the prayer the pastor opened his eyes and saw that the man standing next to him was in tears – despite the fervour of his prayer and the fantastic opportunities for the kids who came to his church. Somewhat surprised, the pastor asked him why he was crying. The man replied, "I am crying because I am angry, pastor. For years I have been a teacher in the local school and not once have you prayed for me. Why does my teaching only matter to God when it's done in church?"[76]

He was right. All too often even those of us who are church leaders divide the spiritual from the secular. We talk about full-time Christian workers as if the rest of us only serve God part time. We talk about a time of worship on a Sunday as if the rest of the week we are dishonouring God or venerating someone else. The Bible knows nothing of this division of life into compartments: all of life is to be lived for God. The narrative literature combines spiritual history with secular history. The psalms combine spiritual honesty with the reality of tough life circumstances and raw emotions. The law lists instructions about worshipping God alongside instructions about working, eating and relating to others. We find the same here in the wisdom literature; the quest for spiritual maturity is applied in the nitty-gritty of life as a son, a father, a neighbour, a friend, a colleague, a wife, a bank manager or a businesswoman.

We inhabit two worlds. Most of us have a natural preference for one or the other. Some people are good at having their feet on the ground, and other people are good at having their head in the clouds. Finding the place where the two best work together is a bit like finding the biting-point when trying to do a hill start in a car with a manual gearbox. Too much clutch onto the things of this world, and we stall in our faith. Too much spiritual accelerator, and again, we stall in our

---

76   Adapted from a story told by Greene, M., 2001, *Thank God It's Monday: ministry in the workplace*, Scripture Union. See also Kandiah, K., 2007, *Twenty-Four: integrating faith and Real life*, Authentic.

faith. The wisdom literature helps us to feel the biting-point, where our spirituality empowers all that we do, seven days of the week.

Once we begin to see that we can be as spiritual in the classroom as we can be at church, then this transforms our idea of worship. If the psalms broadened our idea of worship to show us that we can be honest and public with all our emotions, the proverbs broaden it further to show that we can worship God through the stuff of everyday life – with friendship, science, death, presents, food, work, fairness, justice, reputation and wealth. We worship and honour God through the way we balance our decisions and our devotions.

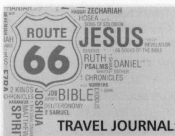

### TRAVEL JOURNAL: Proverbs 31

1. What do you find unusual about this ideal picture of godliness? What is included that you wouldn't have expected? What is excluded that surprises you?

2. How is verse 31 the key to the spirituality of this chapter?

3. Compare the "wife of noble character" of Proverbs 31 to the "fishmonger of noble character" in the story above. What are the similarities between them and how could you interpret this for your life?

4. This supermum picture is not a blueprint for every woman on the planet, but rather a composite picture to illustrate the breadth of ways we can honour God. How does the picture challenge and inspire you?

# Day 4: **Turbo-charged**

I am a sucker for a competition, and very occasionally I am rewarded with a free blackcurrant bush or 10 per cent off entry to a theme park. However, recently I hit the jackpot and won a driving day at the *Top Gear* test track. I knew this was going to be a very different driving experience to my usual trundle along country roads in an ageing people carrier stuffed to the brim with children, books and sweet wrappers. So I climbed out of my own 0–60 mph "if you are lucky" Ford Galaxy and bolted myself into a turbo-charged sports car. What happened next was like having adrenaline pumped straight into my brain! I was still using the basic driving skills taught to me decades earlier by a man in a little dual-control Peugeot 206, but now they took on a whole new dimension as the instructor showed me how to take a corner at high speed sideways!

There is a similar relationship between the orthodox wisdom of Proverbs and the radical wisdom of the other Wisdom books. While Proverbs teaches the foundation of the normal way life works, Job and Ecclesiastes and the Song of Solomon take it to the next level to show how these principles are worked out in the extreme.

## Where is God?

Whereas much of the Old Testament speaks of the great acts that God the redeemer has done to build a covenant relationship with his people, the wisdom literature speaks of what we can do to build a relationship with God the Creator. As William Dumbrell puts it: "The wisdom movement directed its attention to what creation itself implied for human conduct."[77] God created a world with order, consequences and a high level of predictability – the sun always rises in the east (Ecclesiastes 1), and gossip inevitably causes conflict (Proverbs 16:28). But based on the world we see around us alone, sometimes God seems to be missing. This is the conundrum that faces us when we read Job, Ecclesiastes and the Song of Solomon. These three books tackle arguably the biggest challenges to our faith – the experiential crisis of suffering, the existential crisis of senselessness, and the erotic crisis of sexual satisfaction.

---

77   Dumbrell, W. J., 1989, *The Faith of Israel: its expression in the books of the Old Testament*, IVP, p. 228.

## Job and suffering

Job is a man, as innocent as you are likely to find, who becomes the centre of a cosmic conversation between God and Satan about whether his faith is real or just based on the blessings he has received. To prove the point, God allows Satan to test Job to the limit. Job's suffering begins as he loses his family, his possessions and even his health. But while the reader is let into the secret, Job has no idea why his life has suddenly fallen apart. While he is sitting in his desolation, three friends come to "comfort" Job by expounding a number of theories to explain his suffering, based on the logic of Proverbs. Eliphaz virtually cites Proverbs 22:8 word for word when he says: "As I have observed, those who plough evil and those who sow trouble reap it. At the breath of God they are destroyed; at the blast of his anger they perish" (Job 4:8–9).

Despite his friends' sound sermons, Job protests his innocence and holds God to account for how he has been treated. Job is never told why he went through the suffering, but as God eventually addresses Job with a series of questions based around descriptions of twenty animals that demonstrate his wisdom as creator, Job becomes more contrite and God restores his health, wealth and family to him. The message is simple: sometimes bad things happen to good people. We may try to rationalize, even theologize why they occur, but sometimes we will never know. We fear and respect God because of who he is, not because of the blessings he gives us, or because we think we know how the universe works, or because our tidy boxes of doctrine are neatly sewn up. Things won't always work out as we expect because reality is more complicated, and God is more immense than we could imagine.

## Ecclesiastes and senselessness

Ecclesiastes, a shorter book with a more complicated message, contrasts starkly with Job. If Job represents a confused, suffering believer, Ecclesiastes represents a cynical, stoical thinker. Job has intensely personal problems, while Ecclesiastes discusses universal puzzles of existence. The introduction dramatically sets out the big idea of the book: "'Meaningless! Meaningless!' says the Teacher. 'Utterly meaningless! Everything is meaningless.'"[78] The term "Teacher" is a translation of the Hebrew title *Qoheleth*, which can mean "collector"

---

78 Ecclesiastes 1:2.

or "assembler".[79] This nuance shows how the bulk of the book (1:12 – 12:1) is an attempt to make sense of the world but, just like building a Lego model with missing pieces, building life on wisdom, pleasure, riches or reputation is found to be empty and inadequate. Some say that most of the teacher's speeches, like those of Job's counsellors, are to be considered examples of false ways of thinking about God.[80] But Qoheleth's questioning, wrestling approach is much more humble. The Bible leaves room for this type of intellectual debate, and many people have come to faith by this process of elimination – discovering the meaninglessness of life "under the sun", or without God in the equation. The epilogue reaches very orthodox conclusions: life is best enjoyed in relationship with God, and we will be held to account for how we have lived.

## The Song of Solomon and sexual satisfaction

Many people lose their faith because of terrible circumstances or intellectual challenges, but many are also drawn away from the faith because of sexual cravings and temptations. The fourth book in the wisdom literature shows that the Christian faith is not opposed to the erotic celebration of sex.[81] Again, this explores a dimension beyond the proverbs, which admit that "the way of a man with a maiden" is too amazing to understand.[82] In the Song of Solomon, the woman's female escorts counter Job's male counsellors, offering helpful advice and encouragement to the bride-to-be. The whole book is a public celebration of the private, recreational side of sexual encounter, not the procreational side of it.[83] But it also warns of the dangers of sexual desire outside marriage. Talk about turbo-charged! This book is raunchy reading.

When you realize that your car is going through a large puddle of water on a motorway, the temptation is to slam on your brakes as hard as you can to proceed slowly through the hazard. However, recognized wisdom

---

79  Kidner, D., 1991, *The Bible Speaks Today: The Message of Ecclesiastes*, IVP, p. 13.
80  This is not to say the Bible is flawed. Rather, just as the Bible accurately records the false promises and lies of the devil's temptation of Jesus in the desert, so the Bible accurately records the bad advice and flawed thinking of Job's counsellors.
81  Some have tried to allegorize the Song of Solomon into a description of a personal relationship with Jesus: "early Jewish and Christian commentators found the sexual descriptions of the song embarrassingly graphic so they reinterpreted the language to make the book speak of a variety of other theological themes." Estes, D., J. & Fredericks, D. C., 2010, *Ecclesiastes and The Song of Songs*, Apollos Old Testament Commentary, IVP, p. 276. The plain reading of the text points to the book as a poetic celebration of sex.
82  Proverbs 30:18–19.
83  See Gledhill, T., 1994, *The Bible Speaks Today: The Message of the Song of Songs*, IVP, p. 33.

is that brakes are not applied at all, as the car is likely to aquaplane and spin out of control. Instead we are supposed to gently take our foot off the accelerator and steer the car through the hazard. When we hit obstacles in our faith, the temptation is to slam on the brakes and drop out of everything we had been doing and give up hope. Instead Job, Ecclesiastes and the Song of Solomon offer us another path: it is acceptable to take our foot off the accelerator and ask questions about our circumstances, our doubts and our sexuality. We are permitted to buy some thinking time so that our faith finds traction in the midst of the struggles and temptations.

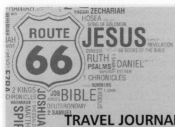

### TRAVEL JOURNAL: Job 4:1–9

1. Eliphaz is one of "Job's comforters", offering anything but comfort to his so-called friend. What is the logic of Eliphaz's position?

2. How does Eliphaz's speech relate to the wisdom we have been reading about in Proverbs?

3. What is right about what Eliphaz says? What is wrong with applying it simplistically as Eliphaz does?

4. Job's comforters show us the dangers of oversimplifying complex issues. How can we avoid making the same mistake?

# Day 5: **Connections**

In the middle of the field, in the middle of the night, lay a dad and a daughter staring up at the sky. They propped themselves up in the damp grass, clutching their mugs of steaming hot chocolate in a bid to keep warm. In the pitch black all they could see were the stars and all they could hear were their own giggles. Suddenly a shooting star blazed across the sky and was instantly gone. Over the next twenty minutes maybe ten more meteorites burned up in the earth's outer atmosphere, each one briefly captivating their audience of two in the field, giving them a memory that would last a lifetime and connecting them with each other, with the universe and with the Creator God.

## The wisdom of God revealed in nature

Unlike a cheap suit, that looks good from a distance but on closer inspection reveals wonky stitching and bad-quality fabric, the universe is wonderfully made, from whatever distance and whichever angle you look at it. God's creative power satisfied Job in his crisis, and Proverbs also ends with an invitation to marvel at God's handiwork (see Proverbs 30:22–31).

Throughout wisdom literature there is a delight in seeing God at work in his world: in the flight path of an eagle,[84] the storage plans of ants,[85] the adaptability of the habitat of small furry mammals or the co-ordination of a swarm of locusts.[86] Reflecting on the complexity and intricacies of nature is supposed to point us to God.

If three of the biggest challenges to faith are questions of suffering, senselessness and sex (as we saw yesterday mirrored in Job, Ecclesiastes and the Song of Solomon), the fourth challenge is often the question of science. Many perceive science, the study of order in the universe, to be opposed to Christianity, but we see here that wisdom literature encourages believers to engage in scientific reflection on the created world as a pointer to the powerful and wise Creator God.

Studying the world certainly helps us to appreciate the wisdom of God, but the proverbs hint at another, fuller way that God's wisdom can be seen. It is an additional piece of the puzzle of creation that would certainly have helped Job and the author of Ecclesiastes. By reading the

---

84   Proverbs 30:19.
85   Proverbs 6:6–8.
86   Proverbs 30:27.

wisdom literature in the light of the New Testament, we see that Jesus himself is the wisdom of God.

## Wisdom – revealed in Jesus

Proverbs 8:22–31 prophetically points to Jesus when it personifies wisdom, saying:

> *The Lord brought me forth as the first of his works,*
> *before his deeds of old;*
> *I was appointed from eternity,*
> *from the beginning, before the world began…*
> *I was the craftsman at his side.*
> *I was filled with delight day after day,*
> *rejoicing always in his presence,*
> *rejoicing in his whole world*
> *and delighting in mankind.*

We could helpfully compare this with the opening verses of John's Gospel, which uses another term for wisdom – *Logos* – translated as "the Word" to introduce Jesus:

> *In the beginning was the Word, and the Word was with God, and the Word was God. He was with God in the beginning. Through him all things were made; without him nothing was made that has been made. In him was life, and that life was the light of men.*

## Wisdom – seen in creation

We have seen already in this book that Jesus is the climax of the biblical story, he is the fulfilment of the law, he is the perfect prophet and he is the Son of David, the poet-shepherd King. He is also the one "in whom are hidden all the treasures of wisdom and knowledge".[87] Jesus is the wisdom of God because the whole of creation is his handiwork; he made it and he sustains it. It comes as no surprise, then, that he knows where fish can best be caught, how to provide for thousands with only a few loaves of bread, how to walk on water, command storms to stop and rid bodies of diseases.

---

87  Colossians 2:3.

## Wisdom – worked out through a person

Jesus, as the wisdom of God made flesh,[88] is the supreme worked example of the wise life. Whether it is countering the devil's attacks in the wilderness with wise use of Scripture, or dodging the trick questions of the Pharisees, or avoiding the temptations that are common to all people, Jesus gives us a model of the art of living beautifully.

## Wisdom – passed on through words

Jesus adopts the "two ways to live" guiding principle which kicked off the book of Proverbs. In Matthew 7 alone we see that he teaches wisdom by comparing the narrow and the wide gates, the true and the false prophets, the good and the bad trees and the wise and the foolish builders.[89] Some of Jesus' shorter sayings are reminiscent of the proverbs and all his teaching offers us wisdom for life.

## Wisdom – that surpasses understanding

Jesus also helps us with the more radical wisdom of Job and Ecclesiastes. In Job we see an innocent man facing physical affliction and the scorn of the religious experts in order to vindicate God's honour. So too the innocent Christ suffers and dies on a cross while the religious leaders of his day, who can't fit Jesus into their closed theological framework, mock and scorn him. In Ecclesiastes we see how the writer struggles with the problem of the meaninglessness of life and death in this world. Jesus' life and death and resurrection answer that longing by showing a meaningful life, a meaningful death, and a hope beyond the grave.

These connections between the Creator God, the Messiah Jesus, the words of the Bible and the lives we live enable us see how the truth of the wisdom literature has passed the test of time, and can help us to navigate life with the Bible.

---

88 John 1:1–18.
89 See Carson, D. A., 1994, *The Sermon on the Mount: An exposition of Matthew 5–7*, Paternoster, pp. 124ff.

**TRAVEL JOURNAL: Proverbs 8**

1. According to this chapter, what is the connection between wisdom and the created world?

2. What makes you think this could/could not be a prophecy about Jesus? (Compare this passage with Colossians 1:15–17.)

3. What echoes of Jesus' teaching do you find in this chapter? (Compare this passage with the Sermon on the Mount.)

4. How has the truth of these verses passed the test of time? Why does it still have so much to teach us?

# Small Group Study 4
# **Living discerningly with the wisdom literature**

In pairs, write down as many common proverbs as you can think of in two minutes. Why are they so popular in our everyday language?

"A proverb is a short sentence drawn from long experience" (Miguel de Cervantes). Discuss.

Take a look at the following list. Which of these proverbs are not in the Bible?

- ⊕ Waste not, want not.

- ⊕ Practice makes perfect.

- ⊕ Moderation in all things.

- ⊕ Time is the great healer.

- ⊕ Money is the root of all evil.

- ⊕ Cleanliness is next to godliness.

- ⊕ You can't judge a book by its cover.

- ⊕ God helps those who help themselves.

- ⊕ All good things come to those who wait.

- ⊕ If at first you don't succeed, try, try, try again.

Would it surprise you to discover that none of these are in the Bible? Which of them represent biblical values fairly and which of them distort or contradict biblical values?

With so many proverbs already stored up in our minds, how can we be sure that we are making godly decisions and choices in our lives?

Read Proverbs 3. Make a list of all the benefits of seeking God's wisdom and show how they fit into the four major aspects of life:

**103**

| Our relationship with God | Our relationships with others |
|---|---|
|  |  |

| Our relationship with ourselves | Our relationships with the world around us |
|---|---|
|  |  |

Take a look at the following case studies. How would you decide what to do in these situations? Use Proverbs 15 to help you.

| Your colleague at work is always making critical comments about others in your office. Should you confront him/her? |  |
|---|---|

| A group of teenagers have recently started coming to church, but some people feel offended by their language. What should happen next? |  |
|---|---|

Which do you find easier to relate to – the black-and-white advice of Proverbs, or the way that Job and Ecclesiastes handle the grey areas?

Discuss the decisions you have made in the past week, or are facing in the week ahead. Share the crises you have faced or are facing. How can the wisdom literature help you to live discerningly?

# Week 5: **Living prophetically**

*The prophets and their application to life*

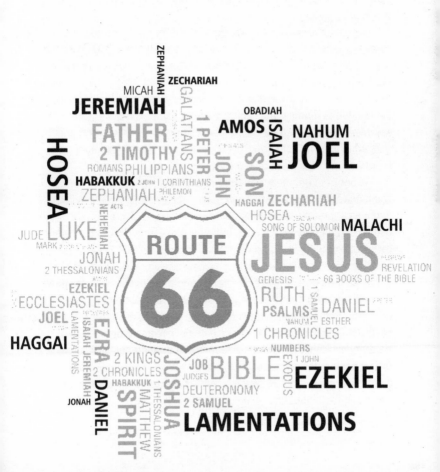

# Day 1: **Viewpoints**

Have you ever noticed that today's news is never today's news? Half of the programme or newspaper is usually devoted to yesterday's news and what happened in the Middle East, or in Prime Minister's Questions or in the courthouses. The other half of the broadcast or broadsheet is usually devoted to tomorrow's news and what might happen in the upcoming election, Wimbledon final or film awards. The speculation is endless, as the experts jostle with each other to predict what may or may not occur. While the reports on what has already happened may prove useful in the future as a record of history, the speculation becomes superfluous as soon as the election or tennis championship or award ceremony is over.

The prophetic literature is not like this. It is not like yesterday's newspaper, filled with speculation about Israel's future 2,700 years ago and superfluous now. Nor is it tomorrow's news with speculation about the planet's future and useless to readers in ancient times. It is not like today's vague horoscope that can be applied to any circumstance, or a ventriloquist's dummy that can be made to say anything we want it to say. Many people mistreat the prophetic literature in these ways and miss what is really going on. This week we will take a closer look at prophecy and how we should read it.

The books of prophetic literature record Spirit-empowered communication from God through human messengers, equally relevant in the past, present and future. As Peter explains it: "For prophecy never had its origin in the will of man, but men spoke from God as they were carried along by the Holy Spirit."[90]

A significant proportion of the prophetic literature is calling God's people to look back to the *past*,[91] reminding them of the promises they had made to God and the covenant God had made with them. The prophetic literature was written to specific people in a specific historical context[92] with references to specific national events occurring in their *present* day. Under the Spirit's guidance and through the Spirit's power the prophets were given insight into *future* events that were often a direct consequence of the people's present-day attitudes to promises in

---

90  2 Peter 1:21.
91  See Green, J. B., 1984, *How to Read Prophecy*, IVP, pp. 60–61.
92  "Biblical prophecy… was addressed by the prophets to their contemporaries." Greidanus, S., 1998, *The Modern Preacher and the Ancient Text: Interpreting and Preaching Biblical Literature*, Eerdmans, p. 229.

the past. The prophets were supernaturally empowered to foretell the invasion of the land, the exile of God's people and their eventual return, or the coming of Christ and details relating to his life. The three key themes of prophetic literature relate to these three time zones.

## The past faithfulness of God

We have a shared history with God's ancient people in that he created us and he rescued us. But the current affairs of Old Testament days, and even some of their fulfilled prophecies, are now part of our history too. The prophecy of the Old Testament is profoundly different from journalistic speculation because what the prophets said really did come true. They relayed God's word and it came to pass. By watching God make promises and then in due course faithfully fulfil them, we are helped to grow in our confidence regarding the other promises in Scripture that are as yet unfulfilled.

## The unchanging moral character of God

Whereas speculation in the newspaper is often based on popularity polls, personality types or probability theory, the prophecies of the Old Testament often revolved around moral attitudes or actions that led to God's intervention of blessing or judgment. God's moral standards do not change, and by seeing the lengths to which he went to impress on his people the way they should live, we too can learn how to please God from reading the prophetic literature. Through the prophets we discover that God is absolutely serious about holiness and justice.

## The future that God intends

Many people scour the prophetic literature to find parallels with our current world history, declaring the rise of China as a superpower, 9/11, or the invention of the barcode to have been predicted in the Bible as immediate precedents of the end of the world. But the Bible is no secret code or horoscope containing Nostradamus-style predictions. The prophetic literature was not written as a time-capsule to be left hermetically sealed and ignored for thousands of years and then opened in the UK in 2021. God used the prophetic literature not only to speak to his people in the Middle East around 700 BC but also for every other time and place in history since. Each of the prophets had an immediate audience in front of them who understood precisely the immediate relevance of what was being said. But by God's grace the message is no less relevant to us.

The easiest way of understanding this is to consider a hiker at the foot of a mountain. Way up in the clouds she sees the peak and for the next few hours ascends the slope, keeping her eyes on the peak. But just as the hiker approaches the top of the mountain, she realizes that she is not quite at the top yet – there is another climb to what appears to be the new summit. When she reaches the top of that peak she realizes there is yet another peak to go, and she begins the final ascent.

As we read the prophetic literature we need to see that we are somewhere between peaks 2 and 3 of history, and that there are often multiple fulfilments of the prophecy. For example, the prophets predict that after the invasion of Israel by the Babylonians there will be a long time in exile followed by a return to the land, as Isaiah states:

> *A voice of one calling:*
> *"In the desert prepare the way for the Lord;*
> *make straight in the wilderness*
> *a highway for our God.*
> *Every valley shall be raised up,*
> *every mountain and hill made low;*
> *the rough ground shall become level,*
> *the rugged places a plain…"*[93]

The prophets were definitely predicting the end of the exile (peak 1); there really was going to be an invasion by a neighbouring country and then after a time the Jews would be allowed to return home. The trouble is, when they came home it didn't seem as grand and spectacular as Isaiah had described.

There were no transformed landscapes or superhighways built in the desert, but rather a slow and small dribble of returnees. There was more to be fulfilled in this prophecy than the physical return of a few Jews to their homeland. As Tom Wright puts it: "Babylon fell, and the people returned. But in Jesus' day many, if not most, Jews regarded the exile as still continuing. The people had returned in a geographical sense, but the great prophecies of restoration had not yet come true."[94] The gospels

93   Isaiah 40:3–4.
94   Wright, N. T., 1996, *Christian Origins and the Question of God, Vol. 2: Jesus and the Victory of God*, SPCK, p. 126.

use the passages that refer to the return from exile to talk about John the Baptist's ministry[95] preparing the way for the Lord Jesus' coming (peak 2). With hindsight we can also now see that they were waiting for God's Messiah to bring restoration to his people, even though they were physically in the land God had given them. Jesus' life, death and resurrection restore God's people back to God, but even the coming of Christ does not completely fulfil the prophecy of Isaiah 40. We still await the final fulfilment when, at the end of time, God will restore all things into right relationship (peak 3).

Before I became a parent, I held a viewpoint that fathers should love their children unconditionally, which would naturally lead to well-balanced, well-behaved children. Six children later, my viewpoint has been tweaked significantly. I now think fathers should do their best to love their children unconditionally, even when their children are not well balanced or well behaved! The advantage of the prophets is that they speak of God the Father's perfect, unconditional love from his unchanging perspective. His love, his discipline, his knowledge of what is going to happen in the course of history, and his faithfulness fill the pages.

I follow all sorts of people who claim to be able to offer a perspective on the past, a commentary on the present and a view of the future. Thanks to Twitter, I follow scientists, journalists, celebrities and doomsayers with their huge variety of viewpoints. But the only one I would trust with my life is the one who spoke truth through the prophets thousands of years ago and who continues to speak today.

---

95   Mark 1:1–4.

**TRAVEL JOURNAL: Isaiah 39:8 – 40:5**

1. What do we learn about God's faithfulness and God's moral standards in these verses?

2. What are the elements of this prophecy that received fulfilment when God brought his people back to live in the promised land in 400 BC?

3. When the Jewish people return from Babylon to Judah, it is more like a slow amble along an overgrown garden path than a high-speed drive along the motorway, as the language of this chapter implies. How does John the Baptist help us to see another level of fulfilment? (See Matthew 3:1–3.)

4. Even with the coming of Jesus, are there things that still remain unfulfilled in this prophecy? How does this inspire us for the future?

# Day 2: **The end of the tunnel**

The father was desperately trying to find his young son, who had been kidnapped and forcibly conscripted into an army as a child soldier. He could hardly imagine what his son had been through – drugged and abused and forced to commit all sorts of crimes and atrocities. After months of searching, the father finally tracks him down, but the boy doesn't even recognize him. His identity has been buried by the mind-altering drugs and by the numbing violence he has witnessed and endured and inflicted. This is the climactic scene in the film *Blood Diamond*,[96] which powerfully portrays the terrible consequences of war, greed and violence. With his son holding a gun to his head, the father pleads with the boy to come home, reminding him of his mother who is waiting for him at home, describing the food waiting on the table for him, and retelling the good times they have spent together. This is not dissimilar to the major theme of the prophetic literature. Story and imagery combine with history to reason and plead with God's people to remember who they are and to come home.

We can see this theme of identity and call right from the outset. The prophetic writings are made up of the fifteen books that carry the name of a prophet – Isaiah, Jeremiah, Ezekiel, the twelve minor prophets, plus Daniel and Lamentations. There is prophecy in other books of the Bible too – characters like Moses, Deborah, Elijah, Elisha, and Samuel all carried the title "prophet". The prophets were from all sorts of walks of life: Ezekiel was a priest living in exile and therefore unable to practise his lifelong calling without the Temple. Amos came from a farming background from the rolling sheep country of Tekoa. Deborah was a prophetess-warrior who led the nation of Israel into battle. Despite their variety, their identity and their call were the same: as God's messengers they were to fearlessly and faithfully speak God's message to God's people.

## The prophets' call by God

If we compare the calling of the prophets Isaiah (6:1–10), Jeremiah (1:1–5), and Ezekiel (1:15–2:10), we see that all three experience a vision that brings them face to face with the overwhelming glory of God. Their common reaction is their immediate sense of inadequacy,

---

96　Warner Bros., 2006, directed by Edward Zwick.

openly recognizing that they have no qualifications to merit having been chosen to be God's mouthpiece for their generation. Their personal calls are a worked and embodied example of how God expects his people to respond – in humility and obedience.

## The prophets' call to God's people

The prophets were sent because God's people had lost sight of their identity and to remind them of their covenant relationship with God. The historical context is set after the nation of Israel had settled in the promised land, but despite the reminders to follow God (Joshua 1 for example) and the warnings of the consequences of disobedience (Deuteronomy 30:11–20 for example), the people became comfortable in their new lifestyle and forgot about God, and therefore about their identity as God's people. God had every right to punish them, but instead he mercifully gave them another opportunity to change – he sent the prophets.

Many people see the prophets as proof of God's impatience, with their stark warnings, strong accusations and fearsome promises of destruction. But in fact the prophets prove God's patience, as he gives every chance for his people to avoid the consequences of their rebellion. Even when they refuse and the punishment is fulfilled, there is always a promise of rescue beyond the judgment. From the darkest pages of the Bible, we see bright pictures of hope and comfort at the end of the tunnel.

This three-stage journey is worth watching out for, as it provides a strong and often repeated structure which can act as landmarks in these books, which are often long and difficult to read.[97]

## Warning

It was part of the prophet's job to spell out how Israel had broken the covenant and to explain that God's judgment was coming as a direct result. Isaiah and Hosea had to challenge Israel's idolatry; Amos challenged their blatant disregard for justice. God's moral standards do not change and these dire warnings must be heard again as a wake-up call to the church today.

---

[97] McConville, J. G., "Prophetic Writings" in Vanhoozer, K. J. (ed.), *Dictionary for Theological Interpretation of the Bible*, SPCK, p. 629.

## Punishment

We may well be shocked at the warnings the prophets gave, but no matter how strong they were, Israel failed to listen to God. What parent wouldn't threaten more and more dire punishments to a child who continually ran into the road? Eventually the punishment must be carried out, in the hope that the child would begin to listen and learn to respond correctly to the stern voice of the loving parent. In the distress of their deserved punishment, God still has the same desire to see his people turn back to him.

## Rescue

There is usually a turning point in the prophetic books where the promise of judgment turns to the promise of rescue. Chapter 40 is the key turning point in the book of Isaiah. The previous chapters are a long, hard slog to read through – but the painful process makes the shift in tone all the more welcome:

> *Comfort, comfort my people,*
> *says your God.*
> *Speak tenderly to Jerusalem,*
> *and proclaim to her*
> *that her hard service has been completed,*
> *that her sin has been paid for,*
> *that she has received from the LORD's hand*
> *double for all her sins.*[98]

Similarly, from the ruins of Jerusalem, Jeremiah promises a time when God will build a new covenant with his people, one that will transform hearts and minds.[99] Despite their sin, God does not give up on his people. He still longs to forgive us, reconcile us and restore us into relationship with him.

God, our loving heavenly Father, calls out to his people through the prophets. He wants to wake us from our trance-like addiction to sin, shaking us out of complacency, and warning us of the dire consequences of hypocrisy, of tunnel vision, of forgetting God, of mistreating others. As we read the prophets we should allow God's righteous anger at sin

---

98 Isaiah 40:1–2.
99 Jeremiah 31:33–40.

to challenge the way we treat sin in our life, our community and our world, and we should face up to the judgment we deserve. But God's last word is not one of judgment, but one of hope. Our lives have been transformed by God's grace to rebels – this is the truth we live by and the truth we should pass on to others.

### TRAVEL JOURNAL: Isaiah 5

1. The joke goes like this: "What do you call a boomerang that doesn't come back? A stick." Similarly, what do you call a vineyard that doesn't produce grapes? What is the tragic mismatch between identity and purpose in this picture?

2. The prophetic call is as much a forth-telling of what God wants of his people as it is a foretelling of what is going to happen to them. What does God want from his people and just how serious is he about this? How are we measuring up in this respect?

3. The chapter seems hopeless. Why is it significant that Isaiah is commissioned in the very next chapter?

4. There is a parallel story of a vineyard in Luke 20, with another violent and tragic ending. How does Jesus build on the Isaiah prophecy?

# Day 3: **Recipe for disaster**

Reality TV shows are irresistibly addictive. The ingredients are simple: firstly, gather together a carefully selected group of misfits who have a propensity for flirting and fighting. Secondly, abandon them in a locked house, on an isolated island or in impenetrable jungle, preferably with very little to nourish their bodies or occupy their minds. Thirdly, leave to simmer and finally serve the results to the viewing public with lashings of product placement and telephone voting.

What I don't understand is why this recipe for disaster is so addictive when eavesdropping on the ensuing conversations is so intensely tedious! It has proved almost impossible to get contestants to talk about anything apart from themselves and their relationships with immediate friends and family. Nobody seems to have even the remotest interest in world affairs, politics, arts and culture, or even the workplace they have left behind.

In reality some churches follow the same recipe. Gather together a group of spiritual misfits who have a propensity for gossiping and grumbling. Abandon them to endless church meetings, isolated from the rest of the community or surrounded by impenetrable jargon, with very little to do but have more meetings. Leave to simmer and serve up weekly on a Sunday with lashings of preaching and sung worship. This too is a recipe for disaster, often leading us to fight with each other instead of working together.

The problem is that when we read the Bible we can have the same tendency as the participants on the reality TV shows: we are only interested in how the passages can be applied to our lives, our needs or our circumstances. It is much harder to be inspired to think through and act upon the implications of what the Bible says concerning bigger issues like global politics, the environment or the workplace.

As a small nation surrounded by ancient superpowers such as Egypt, Assyria and Babylon, we can imagine that the people of God received great comfort from knowing that God was "on their side". But we see throughout the prophets that trust in God degenerated into presumption on God. God's chosen people began to assume that they received diplomatic immunity from all prosecution and persecution, and so it didn't matter how they lived, or how they responded to the terrible things that were going on inside or outside their borders. We know from our own lives how easy it is to have the same short-sighted, self-centred presumption on God.

The prophets step in to refuse to allow God's people to domesticate God or become detached from the wider world.[100] To a people guilty of approaching God as though he were a tame tabby-cat, the prophet Amos shocks his listeners by describing God as a fierce, roaring lion.[101] The prophets tell God's people that instead of worshipping idols and feeding their own greedy egos, they must pass on the blessings they have received from God to the poor and needy and to the surrounding nations, or else they will be punished. The nations that Israel were called to bless ironically became the very means through which God brought the judgment of exile and captivity. This caused Habakkuk one huge problem: it was the "inactivity of God in the face of unrelenting evil"[102] that kick-started his prayer of complaint. This book of prophecy is a prayer conversation between the prophet and God as he complains about God's use of a very wicked pagan nation to judge the lesser evil of the injustices of his own people. But God's recipe for disaster was ultimately a recipe that would benefit the whole world: "For the earth will be filled with the knowledge of the glory of the LORD, as the waters cover the sea."[103] This is just one example of how the prophetic literature forces us to look beyond our own needs and circumstances to God's bigger picture of the world and his plans for his universe.

But looking out at the world does not make for easy viewing, and this was true then as now. The prophets are full of detailed descriptions of barbarities that were occurring in their time. It is not surprising we don't enjoy reading the prophets when we are confronted with the indiscriminate slaughter of children or the mutilation of pregnant women or the deliberate torture of slaves. Grievously, these are no horror stories from a bygone era of inhumanity – the crimes that are talked about in the Old Testament still occur in places around the world. How does God feel about this? Who is responsible? Who will be held to account? The prophets hold the answers.

---

100 Robert Ekblad argues: "Domesticating of God and his scriptures resulting from isolationism is the most destructive pitfall inhibiting liberating reading of the Bible… Hidden or consciously embraced theological assumptions or other presuppositions influence our interpretation causing us to automatically interpret along traditional lines. Left unchallenged these will cause us to consciously or unconsciously look for evidence to support our ideas." Ekblad, R., 2005, *Reading the Bible with the Damned*, Westminster John Knox Press, p. 2. Ekblad's solution is to deliberately study the Bible with a different background – denominationally, culturally, economically – as this will help us see each other's blind spots and attempts to domesticate God.
101 Amos 1:1–2.
102 Smith, R., 1984, *Word Biblical Commentary: Micah–Malachi*, Zondervan, p. 96.
103 Habakkuk 2:14.

If we have a tendency to read the Bible without referring to the world, we also have the opposite tendency – to look at the world without referring to the Bible. When we hear about ethnic cleansing, terrible earthquakes, and awful statistics of infant mortality, we wonder where God is in all of it, and we even doubt whether he cares.

The prophets clearly show us how God feels about injustice.[104] They leave us in no doubt that he does not shut his eyes or look the other way, but sees and feels the pain and he hates it with a vengeance. But God speaks to the root of the problem: his people, who are supposed to be actively combating the injustices of the world, are actually too busy to bother – usually because they are in meetings.[105]

The leaders of our local church are always lamenting that so few people seem to be interested in attending prayer meetings. That is not the problem Isaiah faces when he looks at God's people. God describes a group of people who were fervent and urgent in regular prayer that involved fasting and listening to God's voice. Nevertheless, God speaks forcefully to his people about their spirituality in the book of Isaiah. He does not tell them that if they prayed harder or fasted more often they would see spiritual breakthrough. In fact he describes them as rebellious and sinful, and challenges his people to stop the pretence of prayer and fasting, and instead to do something that will make a difference. God asks that we mirror his abhorrence of evil and join in his mission to eradicate the injustice and suffering around us. The prophets refuse us the possibility of just praying about poverty and injustice or even fasting for a better world. They call us to be active. While we might feel like blaming God for the problems of the world, he lands the responsibility right back on our shoulders and calls us to account and to action.

We cannot claim ignorance about the atrocities of the world, as the superhighway of news gives us virtually instant access to every breaking disaster. But instead of feeling incensed, outraged, spurred into action or empowered, we often feel helpless and powerless in the face of terrible tragedy. But we are not off the hook. The same chapter in Isaiah that calls the church to think globally and set the oppressed free and unloose the chains of injustice shows us that one way to do this is to act locally – clothe the naked, feed the hungry and shelter the wanderer. Jesus echoes Isaiah's challenge in the context of God calling us to account at

---

104 See Haugen, G. A., 1999, *Good News about Injustice: A Witness of Courage in a Hurting World*, IVP.
105 Isaiah 58; see also Isaiah 1:12–20.

the end of time: "whatever you did for one of the least of these brothers of mine, you did for me".[106]

Church is not a glorified reality show and we cannot afford to worship Jesus as the hope for all the nations on the one hand, while living self-absorbed, inward-focused lives on the other. Reading the prophets will recalibrate our idea of worship from what we do inside our church buildings to what we choose to do for the homeless people of our neighbourhood, for the poor people of our nation, and for the oppressed people of the world.

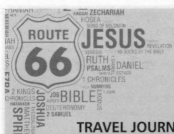

### TRAVEL JOURNAL: Amos 1:3 – 2:16

1. Having spoken out against the sins of all the nations around Israel, God now turns his attention to his people. What is it they have done wrong?

2. God has clearly commanded his people to sing and offer sacrifices, so why does he hate his people's worship services?

3. How do you think God feels about the worship services of your church?

4. Inspired by this passage, write down three practical steps you could take personally and your church could take collectively to make sure your worship is not despised by God?

---

106  Matthew 25:40.

# Day 4: **Wrong direction**

There are many jobs I hope I never have to do. For example, I could never follow in my grandfather's business of hunting the bears and tigers that got the taste for human blood and were threatening the villages of northern India – even a mouse or a large spider in the house makes me afraid. I could never become a bomb disposal expert, as I am the sort of person who turns everything off at the fuse hub before changing a light-bulb. And since I struggle even to return phone calls, I am sure I couldn't have been an Old Testament prophet, as they were given some really tough messages to deliver.

Hosea was asked to go and marry a prostitute and then to chase after her and forgive her when she had committed adultery. Ezekiel had to lie on his right side for 390 days to symbolize the years in exile that the northern kingdom of Israel would endure and then lie on his left side for another 40 days to symbolize the years in exile that the southern kingdom of Judah would face. Jeremiah had to wear a wooden yoke around his neck[107] and Isaiah had to walk stripped and barefoot for three years![108] God in his creativity devised some really unusual and visual ways to make sure that the message of the prophets was effectively communicated through words and actions. The purpose of this was to demonstrate that the people of God were called not just to respond to God's message in words, but to practically and actively and obediently live it out in both public and private. As John Goldingay puts it: "The demand of God for a devotion which expresses itself in total obedience may mean one has no private life. In a sense one has no basic human rights at all."[109]

The prophetic literature therefore contains some strange stories that are supposed to seize our attention and our allegiance. But the strangest of all the prophetic books has to be Jonah, who is swallowed whole by a whale,[110] vomited onto enemy territory and driven to depression by a rogue worm. But this short and strange book can teach us a lot about the nature of genuine prophecy.

---

107 Jeremiah 27:2.
108 Isaiah 20.
109 Goldingay, J., 1994, *God's Prophet, God's Servant: A study in Jeremiah & Isaiah 40–55*, Paternoster Press, p. 23.
110 "Bold would be the man who ventured to say that this series of happenings was impossible, for who can limit the omnipotence of God and say categorically that any could not happen. Not impossible but improbable is how they strike the ordinary reader. What if the author meant to arrest our attention and focus it on his message by means of a string of improbabilities." Allen, L. C., 1976, *The New International Commentary on the Old Testament: The books of Joel, Obadiah, Jonah and Micah*, Eerdmans, p. 176.

First of all, there is an interesting structure[111] to the grand sweep of the book that helps us to identify the main themes through symmetry and repetition.

| | |
|---|---|
| Jonah on the run (1:1 – 2:10) | Jonah on the job (3:1 – 4:11) |
| Jonah's first commission (1:1–3) | Jonah's second commission (3:1–3) |
| Jonah and the sailors (1:4–16) | Jonah and the Ninevites (3:4–10) |
| Jonah's gratitude for his own rescue (1:17 – 2:10) | Jonah's anger at the rescue of the Ninevites (4:1–11) |

Jonah uniquely offers us an insight into life as a prophet by showing us an anti-example. Initially he fails to deliver the message God has given him, running off in the opposite direction. Subsequently he fails to embody the message of forgiveness that God has given him, by complaining and sulking about God's graciousness.

The brutal honesty of the Bible is encouraging. It helps me trust it as a book for real, imperfect people. Jonah is called by God to go and deliver a message of God's interest in the evil international superpower of his day, Assyria. Being called to go and minister to its capital city, Nineveh, was as unattractive a proposition as being called to go and bless Berlin during the Second World War. When Jonah messes up the first time by boarding a ship going in the opposite direction to Nineveh, God does not fire him or abandon him, but relentlessly pursues him, rescues him and recommissions him. This time Jonah obeys, goes to Nineveh, and delivers his simple message: "Forty more days and Nineveh will be overturned."[112] The response of the pagan Ninevites is truly incredible. They demonstrate repentance of a depth and scale unparalleled in the prophetic literature. When heavyweight prophets like Isaiah and Jeremiah prophesy, no one seems to listen. But when spineless Jonah

111 Adapted from Baker, D. W., Alexander, T. D. & Waltke, B. K., 1988, *Obadiah, Jonah and Micah: An introduction and commentary*, Tyndale Old Testament Commentaries, Vol. 26 (105), IVP.
112 Jonah 3:4.

preaches, we are given an account of total national repentance. Instead of delighting in this, Jonah waits in vain to rub his hands over the destruction of this pagan city. God speaks to Jonah a third time, this time using a greedy worm to teach him a lesson about grace, challenging his affection for a plant by contrasting it with his lack of compassion for a whole nation.

The book of Jonah is unique in that the prophet fails to do what we expect of him, and because everybody else does exactly what we don't expect. The sailors fear God despite Jonah's terrible testimony, and the Ninevites repent. Gordon McConville notes: "The only canonical instance of repentance following a prophet's preaching is that of Nineveh to the judgment oracle of Jonah... otherwise the prophetic books testify to inevitable judgment due to persistent sin."[113]

This stark comparison in the prophetic literature between the non-response of God's people compared to the right response of outsiders is mirrored throughout the New Testament. While the Jewish people on the whole reject Jesus, the gospel writers and the apostles cite example after example of Gentiles coming to faith: a Samaritan woman, a Roman centurion, a Canaanite mother, an Ethiopian eunuch and all the social misfits and unclean outcasts you could ever dream of.

We often struggle with the ferocity of the language of the Old Testament prophets, but they are facing a tough audience who ultimately will refuse to follow God. All the stops are being pulled out to persuade them to be faithful, but eventually faith is found exactly where we least expect it. From the anti-example of Jonah, we see that the prophets are trying to keep us moving in the right direction, never underestimating God's grace – either in our own lives despite our failings, or in the lives of the people we would never expect to find faith.

---

113 McConville, J. G. in Vanhoozer, K. J. (ed.), 2005, *Dictionary for Theological Interpretation of the Bible*, SPCK, p. 630. Reproduced with permission of The Licensor through PLSClear.

## TRAVEL JOURNAL: Jonah 4

1. How does the story of Jonah help us to understand the travesty of the failure of the nation of Israel to be a light to the Gentiles?

2. How does the story of Jonah help us to understand the extreme lengths to which the other prophets go to elicit repentance?

3. How does the story of Jonah highlight your own attitude to being part of God's mission?

⊕ I am resisting God's call on my life to serve him.

⊕ I am grateful when God rescues me but my memory is short and I find it hard to pass grace on to others.

⊕ I am more likely to care about the luxuries in my life than the salvation of lost people.

4. How does the story of Jonah highlight any problems in your church?

⊕ We are more concerned to please the Christians than reach the lost.

⊕ We find ways of ignoring God's clear word to us.

⊕ We live as if those who believe differently to us have nothing to teach us.

# Day 5: **Long way round**

It was a long way to go to send a message. But Nick Newcomen drove 12,238 miles in 30 days, logging his position with a GPS tracker so that if anyone were to follow his progress on Google Earth, they would see that he had scrawled the words "Read Ayn Rand" in honour of his favourite author. Driving past Newcomen's car on the motorway, nobody would have guessed what was going on, but as the news spread from Google's perspective, the papers reported this as the largest message that had ever been written – three words scrawled over thirty US states.

It was a long way to go to send a message. But God, over thousands of years, wrote a message about his Son that spanned 31,173 verses of Scripture. Sometimes as we read the verses in the prophets, it can be hard to see the big picture of what is going on. But from the lofty perspective of the New Testament we can see that "Follow Jesus Christ" is, in fact, truly the largest message that has ever been written. There are two key ways the prophets write their message about Jesus:

## The prophets themselves point to Jesus

We have seen this week that Jonah was a resistant prophet, and that Isaiah, Ezekiel and Jeremiah were hesitant, all too aware of their own unworthiness before a holy God. There are also other prophets in Scripture whose back-stories are far from perfect. In Deuteronomy Moses is identified as the greatest prophet,[114] the man the Lord knew face to face, and who performed awesome deeds in Egypt and before all Israel, but even Moses' shortcomings are recorded in the Bible – he murdered, he argued with God, and he hit the rock after he was told not to. When Jesus comes, however, he embodies God's message perfectly, he knows God the Father intimately and works wonders that make Moses' miracles pale into insignificance. The writer to the Hebrews put it this way:

> In the past God spoke to our forefathers through the prophets at many times and in various ways, but in these last days he has spoken to us by his Son, whom he appointed heir of all

---

114 Deuteronomy 34:10–12.

*things, and through whom he made the universe. The Son is the*
*radiance of God's glory and the exact representation of his being,*
*sustaining all things by his powerful word.*[115]

The prophets tried to embody the messages they had to deliver on God's
behalf, but only Jesus managed it perfectly: he is the perfect messenger.

## The prophets' message points to Jesus

The prophets' call to repentance is at the heart of both John the Baptist's
and Jesus' teaching,[116] highlighting perfect continuity between Jesus'
teaching and that of the prophets. Jesus begins to show us how the Old
Testament was pointing to him, and he cites many passages from the
prophetic literature to evidence his claims. At the beginning of his public
ministry, Jesus goes into a synagogue and reads from the book of Isaiah,
identifying himself as the fulfilment.[117] When criticized by the ritualistic
Pharisees for hanging out with sinners, he challenges them to go and read
Hosea 6:6: "I desire mercy, not sacrifice."[118] Not only is Jesus the perfect
messenger – he is also the message.

The authors of the gospels, with the benefit of hindsight, write Jesus'
biography, adding in the footnotes some of the prophecies that Jesus
fulfilled. If even the followers of Jesus who had seen him face to face
came to a more profound understanding of Christ through reading these
ancient prophecies, there is great reason to believe we will benefit from
them. Reading the prophets in the light of the New Testament, we see, for
example, that the Messiah Jesus would be born of a virgin,[119] preceded by
a messenger,[120] would have to flee to Egypt and return,[121] that his teaching
would be misunderstood by many,[122] that he would enter Jerusalem on a
donkey,[123] and that he would be crucified alongside sinners.[124] All these
prophecies uttered hundreds of years before Jesus came were fulfilled
perfectly, helping us know that the details of Christ's life were no accident.
The clarity of the Old Testament prophecies has helped many sceptics find
that Jesus really is the Messiah, God's promised rescuer.

---

115 Hebrews 1:1–3.
116 See Matthew 3 and 4.
117 Luke 4:20–21.
118 Matthew 9:13.
119 Isaiah 7:14.
120 Malachi 3:1.
121 Hosea 11:1.
122 Isaiah 6:9.
123 Zechariah 9:9.
124 Isaiah 53:12.

For those of us who already believe, seeing Jesus in the prophetic literature helps us on three fronts. First of all, we can deepen our trust in God, knowing that he keeps his promises. Secondly, we can learn to be patient with God's promises, realizing that it took 700 years for most of the prophecies about Jesus to be fulfilled. Thirdly, we understand that God is unchanging; he plans millennia in advance just so that we can see Jesus.

It was a long way to go to collect a message, but the government official made the 2,500-kilometre trek from Ethiopia to Jerusalem because he had read something in the ancient Jewish prophetic literature that he could not get out of his mind. As he read a man came alongside his chariot and offered to explain it to him.[125] So it was that Philip led an evangelistic Bible study on Isaiah 53 and showed how it was all about Jesus. God has gone to incredible lengths to give us the Scripture and he will also give us opportunities to pass the message on: *Follow Jesus Christ.*

---

125 Acts 8:26–40.

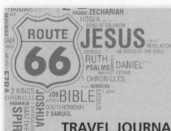

**TRAVEL JOURNAL: Zechariah 11:4–17**

1. Jesus, like Zechariah, is pictured as a shepherd. What are the similarities and differences between the two shepherds?

2. As well as the parallels between messengers, we also see that Zechariah prophesies details of Jesus' betrayal. Read Matthew 26:14–16 to see the significance of thirty silver coins. How does Zechariah's story underline the paltry sum for which Judas betrayed the Son of God?

3. Read Matthew 27:6–10 to see the significance of the potter's field. How does Zechariah's story help us to understand the guilt related to Judas' betrayal?

4. How does the Zechariah story help us to understand and appreciate Jesus as our Good Shepherd?

# Small Group Study 5
# Living prophetically with the prophets

Begin the study by dividing up some of today's newspapers and asking members to cut out articles or pictures that they find challenging as Christians. It might be the story of a natural disaster, an injustice, an environmental issue, a religious article, a celebrity lifestyle column or a piece about asylum seekers. Display them on a coffee table, and ask why these stood out. Imagine what you would say to the people and journalists involved if they were stood before you.

Malachi is a book that stands at the doorway between the Old Testament and the New Testament. It was not written during a major crisis in Israel's life and some would say it was a book written to challenge the middle-class values of a settled people.

Read through Malachi 3 and find parallels between the world of the text, and the world of today. Use the articles on your coffee table as illustrations.

What do these verses imply about what has made God angry with his people?

| Verse | What is God angry about? |
|-------|--------------------------|
| 4     |                          |
| 5     |                          |
| 7     |                          |
| 8     |                          |
| 13    |                          |

Find examples of how this passage calls God's people back to faithfulness to the covenant. Can you think of any Old Testament laws that this passage reminds you of?

How does this passage challenge our self-absorption, our preoccupation with purely private devotions, and the division between worship and action or praise and politics?

This passage seems to foretell a future judgment, but also a future rescue. Identify the two futures. Are any parts of these prophecies fulfilled in the New Testament?

Which metaphors stick in your mind as you look at this passage? Use the images from this passage and the images from the table as the basis of a prayer of confession to God for you, your family and your church.

We know how God feels about the state of the world around us and about the state of the church. He has also entrusted us with information about what will happen in the future. How can we begin to use our imaginations to make a difference to the world around us?

# Week 6: **Living infectiously**

The gospels and their application to life

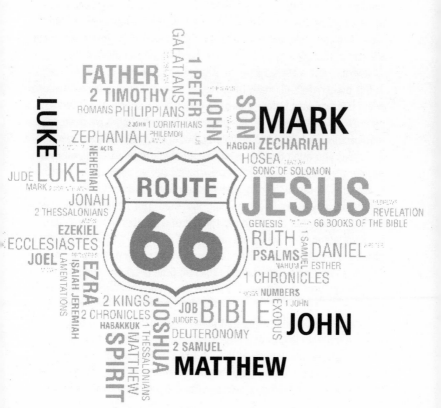

# Day 1: **Used cars**

My wife can't remember the make and model of the first car she drove. However, I have gleaned certain details about it over the years. It was brownish-grey in colour with patches of orange rust. It had a choke that needed to be pulled out just the right amount – too little and the engine would splutter and stop, too much and the engine would drown and then stop. It had an antiquated climate-control system that involved winding a lever to open and close the window. The heating system was a glove-box that actually contained gloves. And if she wanted music, she just had to sing.

Once upon a time that car had been brand new, top of the range and somebody's hard-earned pride and joy. But there is no way my wife would consider going back to her old vehicle. She is now spoilt with the comfort of a car with electric windows, heating, a CD player and many more added extras! Sadly, this is the way many people feel about the Bible. The comforts of the New Testament make the Old Testament seem old and outdated, and inconveniently hard work to understand.

It would not really surprise me if some of you begin to read this book at this point. After all, many of us buy or carry Bibles that have obviously never been opened before that page which has just two words written on it: "New Testament". On the other hand, maybe you have been reading this book from the beginning, but at this point you are tempted to stop as you don't feel the need to read any further. After all, many of us hear the gospels and epistles preached week in, week out at church.

Either way, the blank page between the Old Testament and New Testament may as well be a hundred-foot wall. This barrier can give us the impression that everything to the left of it is superfluous and can be disregarded, just like an old rust-bucket of a car sitting in the corner of the used-car showroom. The barrier can also confirm our suspicion that God went on a retreat during the half-time break between the two Testaments, and went through a major personality change or rebranding process.

Whereas we cannot allow that blank page to permit us to discard the Old Testament in favour of the New Testament, neither can we tear out and discard the blank page as though there were a seamless flow. One of the best ways to understand that blank page is to look at the way the four gospels bridge the gap between the Old and New by holding on to the truth and significance of the Old Testament, seeing the God who is the same yesterday, today and forever, and yet also reorienting our minds to begin to see it through a whole new perspective.

The Gospels of Matthew, Mark, Luke and John offer us four biographies of Jesus.[126] Their format is very much in keeping with the way that ancient biographical accounts were written.[127] Much of the same material is recorded in each one (especially the first three),[128] but each writer has a specific audience in mind that affects how the words and events are described and organized. At first glance each gospel begins in a way that feels much like the Old Testament, a deliberate clue from each writer to see how they dovetail the two halves and how they spotlight upcoming themes of their biography.

*Matthew*,[129] in his Gospel, begins with tracing back the family tree and uses his genealogy to link Jesus with the patriarchal line of Abraham, Isaac and Jacob; with the royal line of David and Solomon; and with Israel's leaders during the exile.[130] However, Matthew is also clear that a new thing is happening – Jesus was conceived by Mary and the Holy Spirit. He uses Isaiah's prophecy to bring the two together: the birth of Immanuel – "God with us" – points to Jesus' full humanity and full divinity, underlining Matthew's major theme of Jesus as the long-awaited Messiah.

*Mark* begins his Gospel by immediately quoting from Isaiah, who prophesied the birth of John the Baptist, an Old Testament-style prophet with the predictable call to repentance. Then Jesus is introduced with this same message of repentance: "The kingdom of God is near. Repent and believe the good news!"[131] But this time God the Father and God the Holy Spirit affirm Jesus' unique identity as the beloved Son of God, with

---

126 See the excellent Burridge, R.A., 2005, *Four Gospels, One Jesus?*, SPCK, for a scholarly yet accessible articulation of the differences and similarities between the gospels.

127 Some argue that the format the gospels take, with no time given to Jesus' early life and so much time given to his death, disqualifies them from the genre of ancient biography, but "The content of Greco-Roman biographies also has similarities with the Gospels. They begin with a brief mention of the hero's ancestry, family, or city, followed by his birth and an occasional anecdote about his upbringing; usually we move rapidly on to his public debut later in life… As for the climax, the evangelists devote between 15 and 20 percent of the Gospels to the last week of Jesus' life, his death and the resurrection; similar amounts are given over to their subjects' death in biographies by Plutarch, Tacitus, Nepos and Philostratus, since in this crisis the hero reveals his true character, gives his definitive teaching, or does his greatest deed." Bauckham, R., 1998, (ed.), *The Gospels for All Christians: Rethinking the Gospel Audiences*, T. & T. Clark, p. 122.

128 Matthew, Mark and Luke are known as the synoptic gospels because they use so much of the same source material that they can be seen (-optic) together (syn-). See Blomberg, C. L., 1997, *Jesus and the Gospels: An introduction and Survey*, IVP, pp. 86–95 for more on this.

129 Carson, D. A., 1984, *The Expositor's Bible Commentary: Matthew's Gospel*, Zondervan. This is an excellent introduction to Matthew's Gospel.

130 The Gospel of Matthew was written "to open up to the hearer a sense of its continuity with the whole Old Testament, and its fulfilment of all God's covenant promises from the beginning of time in Jesus Christ." Jackman, D. & Philip, W., 2003, *Teaching Matthew: Unlocking the Gospel of Matthew for the Bible Teacher*, Christian Focus, p. 7.

131 Mark 1:15.

boundless power over demons and diseases. In this way Mark highlights the similarities and also the crucial differences between the prophets and Jesus.

*Luke*[132] kicks off his Gospel with the births of John the Baptist and Jesus, and uses the generation gap to form the bridge from Old Testament to New. John's father Zechariah, in his priestly role, reminds us of another old and childless patriarch – Abraham. Immediately afterwards we are introduced to Jesus' mother Mary, whose song about her pregnancy is filled with echoes of the hopes of the Old Testament. A great revolution is promised when God will bring justice to his world:

> *He has brought down rulers from their thrones*
> *but has lifted up the humble.*
> *He has filled the hungry with good things*
> *but has sent the rich away empty.*[133]

We see references to the historical literature,[134] to the prophetic literature,[135] to the psalms[136] and to the wisdom literature.[137] Luke deliberately gives the impression that the entire Old Testament hope is encapsulated in the tiny baby Mary is carrying – he is the hope of the whole world in embryonic form.

*John*, the master theologian,[138] with the first three words of his biography of Jesus, takes us right back to Genesis 1 and the creation of the whole universe: "In the beginning…" Imagine trying to produce a remix of "God Save the Queen" for the opening of the Olympic Games that honoured Delia Smith or Lady Gaga? Similarly, rewriting the opening paragraph of the Bible so that it revolved around the person of Jesus would have been a profanity to the ears of many Jewish people. But John is at once affirming the Old Testament teaching that God created the world, and also introducing the New Testament – Jesus is the "Word"[139] by which and for which the world was created. John wants

---

132 See Marshall, I. H., 1988, *Luke: Historian & Theologian*, Paternoster, for a fuller introduction.

133 Luke 1:52–53.

134 For example, 1 Samuel 2:1 – Hannah's song.

135 For example, Isaiah 41:8–9.

136 For example, Psalm 103.

137 For example, Job 5:11.

138 See Carson, D. A., 1990, *The Gospel According to John*, IVP, for an excellent overview of John's theology.

139 John at once affirms Jesus as the fulfilment of the Old Testament creation narrative and also as the "Word" or Logos – a key concept in Greek philosophical thought. "The employment of the Logos concept in the prologue… is the supreme example within Christian history of the communication of the gospel in terms understood and appreciated by the nations." Beasley-Murray, G. R., 1991, *Word Biblical Commentary: John*, Word, p. 10.

us to understand that Jesus' birth is so significant that it reinterprets the whole of the Old Testament and has implications for everything that exists.

Finally for today, here are four things to look out for when reading the gospels in the light of the Old Testament:

⊕ *Foundations:* The gospel writers don't usually reference what they considered to be widely recognized foundational knowledge of the Old Testament. For example, when Jesus said, "I am the bread of life", this would have brought immediately to mind God's name "Yahweh" (literally "I am" in Hebrew) and the miraculous provision of manna in the desert.

⊕ *Fulfilment:* Notice where the gospel writers deliberately refer to the Old Testament prophecies. They have to specifically cite the references because their audience may not otherwise see the connection.

⊕ *Framework:* The gospel writers treat the Old Testament like a frame. They pick up on the events, the imagery and the themes and show how Jesus fulfils them. They ask us, now that Jesus is in the picture, to alter our whole frame of mind to accept who he is, and to pledge our allegiance to him.

⊕ *Field of vision:* Finally, the gospel writers want to expand our field of vision. The gospels are full of clues as to how we should now live not only in the light of Jesus' incarnation and resurrection, but also in the light of his imminent return.

**TRAVEL JOURNAL: John 1**

1. Compare John 1:1–5 with Genesis 1:1–4. How many words are direct quotations? How are they relayed to portray Jesus?

2. Where else in John 1 do you see references to the Old Testament? What does each one affirm?

3. How does John's big picture of Jesus challenge those who treat Jesus too casually or who treat Jesus too cautiously?

4. What does a Jesus-directed life look like, according to John 1?

# Day 2: **Donkeys and Beatles**

I love the stories from art exhibitions where the cleaners have accidently thrown away priceless works of contemporary art because they thought they were literally rubbish. I can just imagine the look on the curator's face when he has to explain to the artist that she shouldn't take it as a personal critique of her work that some of his staff mistook it for litter. Interpreting art can be very complex and sometimes we need a bit of help.

Jesus was a master literary artist, and his ubiquitous storytelling mode of preaching is anticipated in the Old Testament[140] and highlighted in the gospels. Mark says of Jesus, "He did not say anything to them without using a parable."[141] Jesus, with all his insight and intelligence and ingenuity, chose to teach predominantly with stories that were simple enough for children to understand but challenging enough to ensure that even sages struggle to live by them. Adrian Plass helpfully describes a parable as "a story that keeps the listener occupied at the front door while the truth slips in through a side window".[142] Pinning down the parables is trickier than it may first appear, and even the disciples had to ask Jesus for help. Today we are going to look at some principles for understanding and applying the parables.[143]

## **LOOK: the obvious meaning is usually correct**

Jesus' clear teaching that we must love our neighbour – whoever they may be – follows the parable of the Good Samaritan. Here is an example of a parable that is simple enough to take in but extremely tough to carry out. Some theologians have got around this problem by turning the parable into a theological code. For example, one of the ancient church fathers, Origen, asserted that the parable was about Adam walking through paradise and coming across the robbers – the enemy. He couldn't be saved by the priest (the Law) or the prophets (the Levite) but only by the Samaritan (who was Jesus himself). He went even further to say that the wounds represented disobedience, and the two coins paid to the innkeeper (the head of the church) were the Father and the Son finally suggesting that The Good Samaritan's promise to return foreshadowed Jesus' own second coming.[144]

---

140 Psalm 78:2.
141 Mark 4:34.
142 Plass, A., *When You Walk*, 1997, Oxford: Bible Reading Fellowship, p. 254.
143 This section draws on the work of Blomberg, C. L., 1990, *Interpreting the Parables*, IVP.
144 Origen, Homily 34.3, Lienhard, J. T., trans., 1996, *Origen: Homilies on Mark, Fragments on Mark*, Catholic University of America, p. 138.

Allegorizing the parable not only results in the original clear message becoming lost, but also now almost any meaning can be imposed by attributing each aspect with a random element. The reader could decide that the four legs of the donkey could stand for the four points of the compass, the four gospel writers, or for that matter, the four members of the Beatles. Origen in this case was wrong – sometimes a donkey is just a donkey!

## LEARN: the obvious meaning is often multifaceted

The opposite extreme of allegorizing a parable is to reduce it to a single truth. In this case we might summarize the Good Samaritan as a command to love our neighbour. But we know that Jesus was perfectly capable of saying that – so why did he also bother with the elaborate story? A clue is found in the preceding conversation between Jesus and an "expert in the law", who is trying to trap Jesus with tricky theological questions.[145] But during the conversation the expert has unwittingly betrayed his misplaced assumptions that he could earn the gift of eternal life, and that Jesus could help narrow down his definition of "neighbour". He was probably hoping for a neat rule along the lines of "You will get to heaven if, twice a year, you invite for evening drinks those neighbours whose front door you can see clearly from your own front yard, and who have invited you for drinks during the past two years – the rest you can ignore." Instead Jesus replies with a story that sets the standard for earning eternal life impossibly high and blows his idea of "neighbour" a million miles out of the water. The parables are not just truth-bombs, but deliberate stories that shock the audience into opening their minds to a whole new perspective. They help us to see life as God intends it – or, as Jesus called it, the "kingdom of God".[146]

## LIVE: the obvious meaning is always challenging

Jesus did not tell the story to help the "expert in the law" become a better expert in the law or enhance his academic expertise. He wanted to engage heart, head and hands and change the expert's whole perspective on life from the grass roots up. Mark Twain is reputed to have said: "It's not the parts of the Bible I don't understand that trouble me, it's the parts that I do." The challenge is to live out the parable of

---

145 See the excellent Bailey, K. E., 2008, *Jesus Through Middle Eastern Eyes: Cultural studies in the Gospels*, IVP, pp. 284ff.
146 The kingdom of God is a powerful and important theme for understanding the whole Bible. See Goldsworthy, G., 1994, *Gospel and Kingdom*, Paternoster.

the Good Samaritan in daily life by loving not just our neighbour, but our enemy. For this we need God's love, grace and forgiveness to be at work in our own lives.

I recently used the parable of the tenants in the vineyard as part of an all-age harvest service. But the more I prepared it, the more I wondered how I was to communicate the harsh realities of greed, torture, conspiracy, murder, fake religiosity and vengeance in front of the children. Parables have been relegated to Sunday school material for far too long, and we must reclaim them and their challenges for the adult audience they were originally directed toward.[147] Then the adventure will begin as we set out on one of the hardest journeys we will ever undertake – putting into practice Jesus' teaching in the parables.

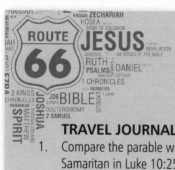

**TRAVEL JOURNAL: Luke 18:18–27**

1. Compare the parable with the parable of the Good Samaritan in Luke 10:25–37. Compare the audience, the questions and responses, and the final conclusions. What are the differences and similarities?
2. What is the obvious meaning of the parable?
3. How do the stories challenge the original audience?
4. Why is it so difficult to put this into practice? What can we learn by our failure to live this out? How can we begin to try to live this out?

---

147 See Novelli, M., 2008, *Shaped by the Story: Helping students encounter God in a new way*, Zondervan Youth Specialities, for a creative way to use Bible stories to help build young people's biblical literacy.

# Day 3: **Soundbites**

I grew up with advertising slogans like these ringing in my ears: "A Mars a day helps you work, rest and play"; "Just do it"; "Vorsprung Durch Technik". I knew the power of the ad men's hook and so I decided I would work on a little advertising of my own. As my son lay sleeping in his cot I would whisper over him. When we were driving along in the car I'd sing to him. I had my slogan stitched into the first scarf I ever bought him. But no matter how many times I recited the words, "You'll never walk alone" to my baby boy, he still chose to follow the lead of his London school friends and, aged four, became an avid Arsenal supporter – an allegiance he still holds to this day. Despite my best efforts to persuade him that Liverpool is the club of champions, I guess that in my home I will walk alone as their fan.

"You'll never walk alone" was the rallying cry from the stands when Liverpool Football Club were 3–0 down at half time in the Champions' League final in Istanbul, but they won the game anyway. It was the moving epitaph written on the thousands of scarves at Anfield when the Hillsborough disaster claimed the lives of ninety-six supporters. It sums up the allegiance of the club and the team mentality of the players when they are operating at their best. Some of Jesus' shorter sayings have the same quality. They get to the heart of the gospel, conjure up memorable, striking images, remind us of our allegiance, sum up big ideas and lodge them into our minds. Examples include sayings such as "It is not the healthy who need a doctor, but the sick"[148] or "The Sabbath was made for man, not man for the Sabbath"[149] or "Greater love has no-one than this, that he lay down his life for his friends".[150] These pithy sayings or aphorisms are not only slogans of allegiance but also act as mental landmarks in Jesus' teaching, as Jesus finds ways to lodge in our minds the often counter-intuitive and always countercultural principles of the kingdom of God.[151]

In Bible times books as we know them did not exist, the scrolls and manuscripts were far too expensive for most people to own, and reading was not a widespread talent. So most people in the oral cultures of

---

148 Mark 2:17.
149 Mark 2:27.
150 John 15:13.
151 See Arias, M., 1984, *Announcing the Reign of God: Evangelisation and the subversive memory of Jesus*, Academic Renewal Press, and Padilla, R., 1985, *Mission Between the Times: Essays on the Kingdom*, Eerdmans, for a very helpful Latin American perspective on the kingdom of God.

the first century would have heard or memorized rather than read the gospels. Parables were easy material to remember, but slogans would travel even faster into hearts and minds and into the viral networks of larger communities, positively infecting people's thoughts, dreams and actions. These slogans are continuing their journey to this very day, as most of us have experienced at some time or other.

On one particular occasion I remember feeling very put out because I was stuck doing a menial job at church, unaided, unnoticed and unable to put my time and gifts to better use. But as I was mumbling under my breath I was hit by a phrase bouncing around in my brain: *"the Son of Man did not come to be served, but to serve"*.[152] Like the proverbs we looked at earlier, Jesus' wisdom for the whole of life had wormed its way into my mind and appeared just when I needed it, forcing me to review my priorities and my attitudes, teaching me humility as I folded endless quantities of notice sheets.

Although these sayings often take on a life of their own, we must remember that each of them is a punchline to some wider teaching. For example, the slogan "you must be born again" makes best sense when understood in the wider context of a conversation Jesus had with an ageing religious expert. Noting when and where they occur can help us to realize their depth, appreciate their beauty and sense their prophetic edge.

Three of Jesus' most cited soundbites teach us about power: "If anyone would come after me, he must deny himself and take up his cross";[153] "If anyone wants to be first, he must be the very last";[154] and "the Son of Man did not come to be served, but to serve, and to give his life as a ransom for many".[155] Each of these sayings has inspired Christians throughout the centuries to worship and follow and sacrifice for their Lord Jesus. However, looking at their contexts reveals a fascinating insight into the problem of power.

All three sayings follow a prediction of Jesus' death and resurrection, and all three precede an embarrassing incident in the lives of the disciples. In Mark 8 Jesus tells the disciples that "the Son of Man must suffer many things… he must be killed and after three days

---

152  Mark 10:45.
153  Mark 8:34.
154  Mark 9:35.
155  Mark 10:45.

rise again",[156] but Peter rebukes him and gets branded as Satan's spokesperson.[157] In Mark 9 Jesus says, "The Son of Man is going to be betrayed into the hands of men. They will kill him, and after three days he will rise",[158] but the disciples are only interested in which of them will be the greatest in the kingdom.[159] In Mark 10 Jesus says, "the Son of Man will be betrayed to the chief priests and teachers of the law. They will… kill him. Three days later he will rise",[160] after which James and John sidle up to him to ask for a promotion.[161]

There couldn't be a greater contrast between Jesus' willingness to be sacrificed for the sake of others and the disciples' short-sighted self-interest. Jesus knew that his disciples would forget what he had told them and fail to take in the significance, so he included the summary soundbites so that in hindsight they would make the connections. These soundbites would remind Christians worldwide of how Jesus' death challenges us to lay aside the intoxicating power of power and follow Jesus' example of giving our lives up for the sake of others. John Stott puts it this way: "Jesus was not speaking only of himself. He was offering a general principle, and went on to apply it to his own disciples who must follow him and like him lose their lives – not necessarily in martyrdom but at least in self-giving, suffering service."[162]

Jesus' soundbites help us to appreciate the gospels, encouraging us to dig deeper, study harder, meditate longer and learn to love Scripture as God's gift of his word to us. And for those of us with little time or bad memories, they inspire us to hold on to key truths that impact our day-to-day lives.

Secondly, these soundbites highlight the centrality of the cross,[163] both as the source of our eternal salvation and as the model for our ongoing discipleship.

Thirdly, they help us to set priorities that are in line with the key themes of the Bible. One of Jesus' most memorable soundbites was "But seek first his kingdom and his righteousness, and all these things will be given to you as well."[164] Pray that these nuggets of Jesus' teaching

156 Mark 8:31.
157 Mark 8:33.
158 Mark 9:31.
159 Mark 9:34.
160 Mark 10:33–34.
161 Mark 10:35–37.
162 Stott, J., 1990, *The Cross of Christ*, IVP, p. 321.
163 Martin Luther, the reformer, went as far as to say: "crux sola est nostra theologia – the cross alone is our theology". See McKnight, S., 2007, *A Community Called Atonement*, Abingdon, p. 52.
164 Matthew 6:33.

would lodge in your memory and inform your heart. Ask that they would have greater sticking power than the advertising slogans you hear each day – so that God can set the priorities for your life.

## TRAVEL JOURNAL: Matthew 6

1. Which phrases in this chapter are well known even outside the church?

2. Often we look at this chapter a section at a time. What is the logic that runs between the sections? How do the well-known sayings act as soundbites summarizing the whole chapter and highlighting an important facet of Jesus' ministry?

3. Central to this chapter is the Lord's Prayer. How does acknowledging God as our holy Father in heaven act as an anchor-point for all the teaching in this chapter?

4. How does understanding the sweep of this chapter help us in applying our faith to our day-to-day lives?

# Day 4: **Skyline**

You'll never hear a bell used more aggressively. If I am in the middle of one of my long cycle commutes across London at the end of a busy day and you are dawdling in my lane gawping at some tourist attraction on the horizon, then do not be surprised if you hear the wrath of my bell. You may well be distracted by the heights of the historic landmarks or the window displays of the famous shops or the face of some celebrity, but this is no excuse. Avoid the temptation to step backwards into clearly marked cycle routes – the ones with a big picture of a bike between lines painted red! Look down occasionally and notice where you are putting your feet before some grumpy, tired cyclist totally uninterested in the buildings or views runs you over!

When it comes to the gospels, my blinkered perspective is often the same as the one I have on my bike. I look down at my favourite lines and details of the story, focus on my own commitments and forget to gaze in wonder at the skyline of the gospels, or notice their key structures. When I take my family to visit London, I change mode from cyclist to tourist and the city takes on a whole new perspective. By doing this with the gospels, we can appreciate the panorama of the bigger picture.

John's Gospel is deliberately structured to help us understand who Jesus is. Seven miracles are matched by seven discourses,[165] and in case we miss the point there are seven "I am" statements in John's Gospel. For example, Jesus explains that he is the light of the world, and demonstrates this fact by giving sight to a man born blind.

John calls the miracles that Jesus performed "signs" because they are more than just demonstrations of supernatural power. They certainly show that Jesus has power over disease, disaster and death, but they also show his concern, creativity and compassion, and they act like motorway signs pointing to evidence that Jesus is the Son of God:

> *Jesus did many other miraculous signs in the presence of his disciples, which are not recorded in this book. But these are written that you may believe that Jesus is the Christ, the Son of God, and that by believing you may have life in his name.*[166]

---

165 Blomberg, C., 1997, *Jesus and the Gospels*, IVP, p. 160.
166 John 20:30–31.

John openly admits that he has not written an exhaustive account of everything that Jesus did and said, but that he has deliberately selected his material to provide a compelling case for the true identity of Jesus, and to help his readers put their trust in him. This selectivity explains why many of the same stories appear in the different gospels but often in a different order or with different details emphasized. According to John, faith in Jesus was never supposed to be a blind leap of faith but an informed step of trust, as the miracles affirm that Jesus is who he claims to be.[167]

The skyline gets busier and busier toward the end of each gospel. Jesus' early years get hardly a mention, his last three years get more attention, and then we are given almost a blow-by-blow account of the last week of his life. Some have gone so far as to say that "the gospels are extended passion narratives".[168] Howard Marshall observes that "of the sixteen chapters of Mark's Gospel, a full six are devoted to the final visit by Jesus to Jerusalem – a visit that culminated in his death".[169] The trial, death and resurrection of Jesus evidence that he is more than a great moral teacher, a mighty prophet or a claimant to the throne of Israel. Jesus' death is clearly central to his mission, and the resurrection is the miracle that most clearly signposts him to be the Son of God, placed as the climactic finale to all four gospels. Jesus really is the way, the truth and the life.[170]

As we read about the miracles of Jesus, we see that they point us to look upward to God and outward at the skyline of the gospels. Here are three ways we can check this:

## Identity

Notice how the miracle reveals more about who Jesus is. There is a powerful moment at the end of John's Gospel where the sceptic Thomas comes face to face with the risen Jesus. Confronted with the walking miracle, all Thomas can do is stand in awe as he recognizes who Jesus really is: "My Lord and my God!"[171]

---

167  See Keller, T., 2008, *The Reason for God: Belief in an Age of Scepticism*, Hodder & Stoughton, for more on this.
168  Kahler, Martin, 1964, *The So-Called Historical Jesus and the Historic, Biblical Christ*, Philadelphia: Fortress, p. 80, quoted in Blomberg, C., 1997, *Jesus and the Gospels: An Introduction and Survey*, Leicester: Apollos, p. 116.
169  Marshall, I. H., 1979, "Jesus in the gospels" in Gaeblin, F., ed., 1979, *The Expositor's Bible Commentary, Volume 1: Introductory Articles*, Zondervan, p. 518.
170  John 14:6.
171  John 20:28.

## Encounter

Discover how the miracle brings you closer to Jesus. Thomas' honest scepticism betrays a widespread attitude. He declares that he cannot have faith unless he not only sees a miracle, but handles the evidence with his own fingers. In the end, however, his faith comes not from physically and forensically scrutinizing the evidence but from encountering the Jesus he knew and loved.

## Faith

Ask how the miracle affirms your faith. Jesus' response to Thomas is to declare blessing on those whose faith comes from encountering Jesus without seeing him. At first glance this may seem like Jesus is talking about blind faith. But in the very next verse John states that his book is written as evidence so that others may believe. In other words, our faith is not blind, it is informed by the trustworthy eyewitness testimony of the gospel writers.

Occasionally on my cycling commute across London I am forced to suddenly stop and get off my bike. On one occasion I spotted Concorde on its last flight making a lap of honour over Buckingham Palace. Once I came across crowds enjoying the band U2 doing a surprise rooftop gig. They were modern-day miracles that forced me to abandon bike bell and mission to Marylebone and simply enjoy looking up at the skyline. This is the effect that the gospel writers want to produce in our lives. As we suddenly come across remarkable, once-in-a-lifetime events in our Bible reading, we have no choice but to lift our eyes beyond the daily grind and revel in the assurance that we know a God who can do the impossible.

## TRAVEL JOURNAL: Luke 5:1–32

1. How does Jesus' identity become public during these four incidents? How does he describe himself in each episode?

2. What amazing transformations happen in ordinary situations in this chapter and how do they point to the life that Jesus wants us to lead?

3. According to verses 20–26, why does faith precede the miracle, and what then is the purpose of the miracle?

4. What does faith in Jesus look like in practice? Scan the passage and see how people react to Jesus.

# Day 5: **Conversations**

The interviewer didn't know what to do. David Blaine, the world-famous showman and illusionist, was on the breakfast TV show being interviewed live in front of an audience of millions. Eamonn Holmes, the presenter, asked multiple questions to try to get Blaine to speak, but all he got were nods and winks and, if he was lucky, monosyllabic answers. Various theories flew around as to why Blaine behaved like that: Was he high on drugs? Was he trying to win a bet? Was he trying to add to his mystique as a magician? Whatever the reason, he came across as aloof and arrogant, as though he was so powerful that he did not need to engage in casual conversation or give anything to the watching public.

What a difference with God. The whole Old Testament tells of a speaking God. He speaks the universe into being. He speaks to his people. He speaks the law through Moses. He speaks through the prophets. And then Jesus comes – the great conversationalist. Jesus speaks to the crowds and to his closest friends. He speaks to the leaders and the lepers, to men, women and children, to socialites, socialists and social outcasts.

We have seen how Jesus speaks to us today through parables, aphorisms, and miracles. Finally we come to take a closer look at the conversations recorded in the gospels. Although they are not spoken directly to us, they are given to us as gifts, offering us a window on the compassion and passion of God, and presenting us with a model of how we can relate to others.

Conversation is often hard work. Have you ever felt that you are trying to get blood out of a stone? Have you ever let something slip you should have kept in? Have you ever found yourself stuck in a conversation you wish you weren't having? Have you ever felt words fail you when a friend tells you a terrible piece of news? Have you ever thought of exactly the right thing to say in an argument, but it is a day too late? There are conversations that I treasure, and those that haunt my darkest memories. Words can be a real opportunity to encourage and bless others, but equally we can embitter and belittle others with just a slip of the tongue.

All too aware of our own shortcomings, we can learn from the master of conversation as we watch Jesus in action in the gospels.

## Look out for the contrasts

The contrasts in conversation highlight the good and bad ways to use our words. The gospel writers make this easier for us by placing contrasting conversations in juxtaposition. Note the contrasts between the comments of the thieves either side of Jesus on the cross;[172] between the nine thankless lepers and the one grateful leper;[173] between the man born blind whom Jesus heals, and the sighted Pharisees who can't see Jesus;[174] between the betrayer Judas and the denier Peter.[175]

## Look out for the context

As we saw before, Jesus' conversations are often linked with a miracle or a festival. For example, Jesus declares himself "the light of the world" during the feast of Hanukkah, a Jewish festival to commemorate God's provision of oil for the temple lights.[176] The conversations of Jesus, like the whole of Scripture, are both human and divine. They are the words of God but spoken into the realities of human contexts. Sometimes when we read the Bible we may miss out on some of the implications of what was being said, as we are removed from the context – we don't always understand the significance of the feasts, or the politics of Palestine, or the beliefs of the different religious groups that try to trap Jesus. If, like me, your knowledge of first-century Middle Eastern cultural practices is pretty non-existent, you will have to rely on good Bible commentaries to help you here.[177] But even without them, being observant can get you a long way. For example, if you look closely you will notice that many of Jesus' conversations took place over mealtimes – there are at least ten occasions just in Luke's Gospel. Perhaps we can learn to take advantage of social occasions to engage in meaningful conversation that would never happen in the daily business of life.

## Look out for the conflicts

Jesus is the master of a wise response. He was constantly being baited and taunted by his enemies who sought to trap him into saying something that would incriminate him. We watch Jesus counter a question with a question, or offer fitting replies under pressure that

---

172 Luke 23:32–43.
173 Luke 17:11–19.
174 John 9.
175 Matthew 26:14–75.
176 John 8:12, 10:22.
177 See the appendix "Tools worth investing in" for some recommended Bible resources to aid Bible study.

silence his enemies. Jesus does not flaunt his intelligence, but speaks without theological jargon or clever techniques of argument. In times of conflict, he is both wise and humble. Finally, in his trial, his silence speaks louder than words.[178]

## Look out for the conversions

Jesus' conversations resulted in conversions. He made time for fishermen and tax collectors, for X-rated adulterous women and for A-list professional theologians. Jesus was delighted to explain the depth of God's love in terms each one would understand. But Jesus did not shy away from telling the hard truths about the judgment of God or the cost of discipleship. The last recorded conversation we have of Jesus is when he is on the cross, a victim facing verbal bullying from the crowds and the religious elite and physical torture from the Roman soldiers. He does not answer back, call down curses or shout out a speech in his own defence. Instead, the gospel writer records that he makes time to listen to the self-confessed criminal next to him and to offer him hope and grace.[179] We have much to learn from the control and compassion and courage of Jesus, and we need to connect them appropriately to the people we talk to each day.

Today I have spoken to a friend who has booked herself in for an emergency mammogram, to a young mum wondering how her child will ever settle in school, to a man who has put himself into debt to set himself up in a risky business, to my wife concerning our plans for half term, and to my neighbour who just had a visit from her father after eight years of the silent treatment. I wonder if I conveyed any of Jesus' compassion and truth in my conversations. I wish I could prepare for tomorrow's conversations ahead of time, but all I can do is reflect on how Jesus treated people and pray that I may become more like him.

---

178 See Isaiah 53:7, "he was led like a lamb to the slaughter, and as a sheep before her shearers is silent, so he did not open his mouth."
179 Luke 23.

## TRAVEL JOURNAL: Luke 23

1. There are three different types of people that challenge or mock Jesus as he hangs on the cross. What is the basis of their challenge to him? How would you respond in that situation?

2. How does Jesus respond to the mocking of the crowds? Read 1 Peter 2:21–23. These verses are a commentary on Jesus' response, and they offer us a model to live by.

3. What does Jesus say and why? Read out his direct speech. How does this give us clues as to what Jesus came to do?

4. How does Jesus' conversation help to guide you in your own contexts and conversations?

# Small Group Study 6
# Living infectiously with the gospels

You may like to discuss this week's small-group questions over a meal.

### Appetizer

"Jesus got himself killed because of the way he ate."[180] Discuss.

How many incidents can you think of in the gospels that are to do with food? Why does Jesus choose to do more teaching over a meal than over a lectern? Think of at least five reasons.

1

2

3

4

5

Which gospel meals are most meaningful to you?

### Main course

Read Luke 24:13–50. Why do you think that, in both accounts, Jesus uses the whole of Scripture and food as evidence that he really has risen from the dead?

In the first account, Cleopas and his friend return immediately to Jerusalem to tell others the good news. In the second account, Jesus has to hold the disciples back from telling everybody. How can we recapture this infectious desire to spread the good news?

How can mealtimes be great places for us to share the gospel with others?

### Dessert

Think about the people you have invited to share meals with you. Read Luke 14:7–24. What are the principles Jesus says we should use for our own dinner parties?

Think about the meals you are going to have this week. What could you do to transform one of them to make it more like one of Jesus' meals? Pray for one another to put these suggestions into practice this week.

---

180 Robert Karris, quoted in Gempf, C., 2005, *Mealtime Habits of the Messiah*, Zondervan, p. 18.

# Week 7: **Living purposefully**

*The epistles and their application to life*

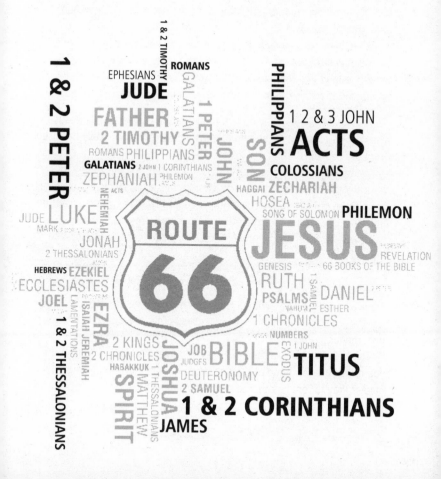

# Day 1: **Hyperdrive**

I will never forget the first time I met the cleaning lady for our student hall of residence at university. She walked into the room and said, "Hello, I'm Glad." I had to bite my tongue hard not to reply, "Glad to meet you." I will never forget the first time I met my brother-in-law during a talk I was giving at his school. He introduced himself muttering, "Sorry, Dennis." I called him Dennis the entire afternoon, until finally he graciously took me to one side and explained that his name was Jon, and what he had tried to tell me was that his mouth was numb from having a filling done at the dentist! Unfortunately most of the time I forget names as soon as the introductions are over, and then spend the rest of the conversation trying hard to recall them and wishing I had paid greater attention.

As we begin this week of looking at the epistles, we will start with the introductions we usually skip over and see how they help set the tone for everything that comes afterwards. Take a look at these five introductions to five different churches written by the same author:[181]

| Galatians | Paul, an apostle – sent not from men nor by man, but by Jesus Christ and God the Father, who raised him from the dead – and all the brothers with me, To the churches in Galatia: Grace and peace to you from God our Father and the Lord Jesus Christ, who gave himself for our sins to rescue us from the present evil age, according to the will of our God and Father, to whom be glory for ever and ever. |
| --- | --- |
| Ephesians | Paul, an apostle of Christ Jesus by the will of God, To the saints in Ephesus, the faithful in Christ Jesus: Grace and peace to you from God our Father and the Lord Jesus Christ. |
| Philippians | Paul and Timothy, servants of Christ Jesus, To all the saints in Christ Jesus at Philippi, together with the overseers and deacons: Grace and peace to you from God our Father and the Lord Jesus Christ. |

181 Paul's letters follow the forms and conventions of the first-century Greek-speaking world. He follows the usual patterns, opening with "A to B, greetings". Then comes an expansion of the basic pattern (e.g., Romans 1:1–7; Galatians 1:1–5; 1 Thessalonians 1:1; Titus 1:1–4), which often points to the specific purpose of the letter. O'Brien, P. T., "Letter forms" in Hawthorne, G. F., Martin, R. P. & Reid, D. G., 1993, *Dictionary of Paul and His Letters*, IVP, p. 551.

| Colossians | Paul, an apostle of Christ Jesus by the will of God, and Timothy our brother, To the holy and faithful brothers in Christ at Colosse: Grace and peace to you from God our Father. |
| --- | --- |
| 1 Thessalonians | Paul, Silas and Timothy, To the church of the Thessalonians in God the Father and the Lord Jesus Christ: Grace and peace to you. |

## The stylistic differences

It is very rare that an envelope comes through my door these days with the address handwritten; although when I spot one I always open it first. Sometimes they contain cards with a brief greeting, sometimes they contain cheques with a curt apology, and sometimes they are, sadly, just impersonal mail shots in disguise. The letters of Paul were proper handwritten, heartfelt conversations and instructions to the local churches he had planted all around Asia Minor. The introductions may look similar by placing them side by side, but this does not mean Paul had done a mass mail-out. Rather, it reveals the culturally standard format of personal correspondence. Paul introduces himself, identifies the recipient, and sends a greeting before getting into the content of the letter. The recognized format of our day is slightly different. We would identify the recipient first, then write the letter, finishing with a greeting and the name of the sender: "Dear Corinthians. Letter. Every Blessing, from Paul." The result is the same – we recognize what the genre is, and some of its context. Grace and peace are always highlighted right at the start to set the tone for the letter. Whether we go on to read criticisms, instructions, prayers, longings or greetings, we understand that Paul's motivation is graciously to see peaceful churches.

## The thematic differences

Because the introductions are so similar, even the smallest differences stand out – and this is intentional, as Paul wants to draw our attention to what will be a key theme of the letter. For example, Paul seems generally to introduce himself as an apostle, but in the letter to the Philippians he introduces himself and Timothy[182] as servants. Paul is

---

182 Paul addresses both 2 Corinthians and Colossians as being from himself and Timothy.

communicating with friends,[183] so he doesn't need to exert his apostolic authority but instead models servanthood. The theme of servanthood, humility and unity is paramount throughout this letter, as we see most clearly in the familiar hymn of praise to Christ the Servant King,[184] which is included as a model of how we should relate to others.

## The contextual differences

Occasionally I receive a text in error, and I always feel in part guiltily embarrassed, and in part intensely nosey as I gain an unsolicited insight into some stranger's life. When I discover that "B" is waiting outside Starbucks for "Maz", my imagination goes into hyperdrive. I picture him in the rain with no umbrella getting cross at the no-show. I imagine he is waiting to propose or elope, or perhaps he is some child kidnapper with evil intentions that have been thwarted by failing to type in the number correctly! I so want to find out what happens next, but recognize this would draw attention to my own crime of eavesdropping. Thankfully, we are allowed to eavesdrop the epistles and be drawn into the action with our imaginations with no shame, in a similar way to when I eavesdrop my wife's phone calls with her sister. I can only hear half of the conversation but I can usually imagine pretty accurately the gist from my wife's expressions, reactions and intonations, and I know well that my wife will fill in the details I fail to guess later anyway. When Jesus returns we will discover everything we would like to know about the context of the letter, but for now there are more than enough clues to help us work out the gist of it.

## The applicational differences

Although we are eavesdropping on a conversation between Paul and a first-century church, we are simultaneously reading a communication from God to us. These letters are written to specific churches in specific cities facing specific challenges and opportunities, and we need to be picking up on all the clues that help us understand the original context. Not every verse is a systematic pronouncement of how our churches should be today,[185] but the theme of the letter, the flow of

---

183 Gordon Fee describes Philippians as a "letter of friendship". Fee, G. D., 1995, *Paul's Letter to the Philippians*, NICNT, Eerdmans, pp. 2–14.
184 Philippians 2:11–15. See Blomberg, C., 2006, *From Pentecost to Patmos: An introduction to Acts through Revelation*, B&H Academic, p. 334, for an excellent literary analysis of the hymn.
185 See McKnight, S., 2009, *The Blue Parakeet: Rethinking how you read the Bible*, Zondervan, for a very accessible exploration of how we decide which parts of the Bible apply just to the original audience and context, and what endures for today.

the paragraphs, the historical background information, and the wider teaching of the Bible will all help us to work out which parts are a window into the particular problems of those first-century churches, and which parts are valuable advice applicable to our twenty-first-century churches.

I remember being introduced to a shy girl in a Bible study in my first week of my first year at university. I had already met a lot of people that week, and I was concentrating really hard on remembering everybody's names. I knew that I would be living and working and praying and eating and staying up late with these people for the next three years of my life and I imagined that I would need all the friends I could get. What I could not have imagined was that I would end up married to that unassuming girl sitting opposite me and that together we would share a lifetime of adventures. When we begin to read the epistles, we are getting to know all sorts of people that we will spend eternity with, not least God himself, whose grace and peace is lavished on every page, and which will uphold us for the rest of our lives.

## TRAVEL JOURNAL: 3 John

1.  Read the book of 3 John. As you listen in to this communication between the apostle John and Gaius, the leader of the church, what can you piece together of the relationship between John, Gaius and the congregation?

2.  Who are the people that are described in the following verses:
    "My children" (4).
    "Brothers" (5).
    "Friends" (14).

3.  How do the descriptions of relationships in the church challenge the way that we relate to each other in our churches?

4.  Why not send a short email, text message or letter to a leader you know today, inspired by the themes of this letter?

# Day 2: **Off track**

I was once travelling back from a research seminar at Cambridge University with a colleague of mine. We continued to debate the minutiae of philosophy and theology as we left the auditorium, as we walked to the train station, as we boarded the train and for the whole of the journey. Finally the cut and thrust of friendly but vigorous debate had to be terminated as the train pulled into the station and we were about to go our separate ways. At this point one of the other passengers on the train approached us and asked: "So how many is it?" Puzzled, we looked at him for some clarification. "How many angels can you fit on a pinhead?"

There was a split second of silence in which you could have heard that pinhead drop, and during which I rapidly relived the debate through his eyes. I realized that from his perspective, we were two combative Christians reinforcing the stereotype that theology was irrelevant to everyday life. Faith, to him, was little more than a professional proof-text ping-pong game, which was about as exciting as waiting for the next train.

Unfortunately many of us experience this tedious tension in our home groups too, when some controversial verse in the epistles crops up and the meeting descends into arguments about homosexuality, headship or hell. The reason we get off track and into hot water is that often we don't recognize the kind of documents we have in our hands. Instead of remembering that the epistles are valuable personal correspondence, we treat them like we would our own mail.

The first thing I do when the postman arrives is sift through the pile of post over a waste-paper basket, dropping the junk mail in without even opening it. Occasionally I will spot a voucher or a competition entry that might be worth rescuing, but some 90 per cent of my mail is trashed immediately. We are often tempted to read the epistles standing over a metaphorical waste-paper basket, looking out for verses that offer us free peace of mind or a good deal on health that we can salvage from the junk around it. This is no new method of Bible reading. The apostle Peter came across people doing the same thing with Paul's letters:

> *Bear in mind that our Lord's patience means salvation, just as our dear brother Paul also wrote to you with the wisdom that God*

*gave him. He writes the same way in all his letters, speaking in*
*them of these matters. His letters contain some things that are*
*hard to understand, which ignorant and unstable people distort,*
*as they do the other Scriptures, to their own destruction.*[186]

I find this insight encouraging, enlightening and frightening. If the leader of the early church struggled to understand some of Paul's letters, there's hope for all of us! It's enlightening because he nevertheless assigns them the same authority as the Old Testament Scriptures, which no Jewish person would do lightly. At the same time Peter's words are frightening because there is a dire consequence if we try to discard or distort Paul's teachings. We cannot pick and mix our way through the epistles, discarding what we don't like – every word is important.

Imagine you received a letter from your Great Aunt Gertrude in which she mentions her geraniums. It would be unlikely that you would enter into a family debate about why Geraniums are an essential part of Aunt Gertrude's identity and have one of the adults in your household write a thesis about why Irises wouldn't have worked for Aunt Gertrude. Something of the nature of the letter she sent would actually be lost with this kind of over analysis.

And yet this is often how the letters of Great Uncle Paul get treated. If, on the one hand, we are tempted to discard the difficult parts like junk mail, the opposite danger is that we are tempted to distort them by too much analysis. A lot of the fights I watch on the blogosphere or hear from pulpits are fights over the interpretation of verses from the epistles. Theology of this sort can be contentious and confusing and is far removed from Paul's true intention, which was to show how good theology can encourage, challenge and unite a church.

The writers of the epistles were not trying to set out a definitive account of the Christian message as the fundamentals of faith for future churches everywhere; they were responding to the pressing needs of churches encountering challenges on the ground. In Romans the main theme is about helping Jewish and Gentile Christians to "welcome one another" and to see each other in the purposes of God. In Corinthians it was about celebrity-based schisms. In Galatians it was about trendy new teaching that was threatening to undermine the gospel, and in Ephesians it was the challenge of multicultural church. Paul balances

---

186 2 Peter 3:15–16.

his responses, calling for unity and the avoidance of "foolish and stupid arguments" (2 Timothy 2:23) on the one hand, but not afraid, on the other hand, to take a stand when he feels the gospel is being compromised (see Galatians 1).

The fact that the early churches faced very diverse and difficult challenges is good news for us in our own church struggles. We see that Paul, through the letters, encourages the Christians, affirms the gospel, and promotes principles of grace and peace, of humility and servanthood, of relationship and respect. We are not supposed to solve all our challenges with Paul's situation-specific teaching, but whatever challenges we do face, we would do well to learn from Paul's attitude.

His attitude is clearly revealed in the prayers which typically follow the introductions in each letter. They are a very personal and intimate expression of Paul's partnership and encouragement. Many of the letters are written from prison (it was probably the only time Paul slowed down for long enough to put pen to paper!), and yet the prayers do not call for his release or for a vigil. Personal comfort came low down on the list of Paul's priorities – more important by far for him were unity, faith and gospel ministry.

There is intimacy, energy and urgency about these prayers and about these letters. This is not a dusty theologian wondering how to confuse as many people as possible with a new book. This is an emotionally intelligent radical activist writing from prison about how the church can continue in God's mission unabated. These epistles can help us set our own priorities, encouraging us to put aside unnecessary controversies and focus on gospel unity, offering clarity to our church vision and our own prayer life and bringing vitality to our Scripture reading. Next time I discuss faith with friends on a train journey, I pray that my fellow passengers will catch something of Paul's contagious love for God and his global church.

## TRAVEL JOURNAL: Philippians 1

1. Imagine you are the young Philippian church facing internal and external problems and that you have just heard your church leader has been imprisoned. How does Paul affirm the church in a variety of ways?

2. What clues are there in this passage about the problems facing the church and what values mark Paul's responses?

3. How does Paul relate personally to the church? What are the indicators of genuine intimacy? How does Paul help the church feel part of God's global church?

4. What aspects of Paul's prayer help us to see theology as vital and active and radical? How can we emulate this in our own prayer life and Bible study?

# Day 3: **Go the distance**

"Do you work – what do you do for a job?" This innocent question is probably asked millions of times a day around the globe. Work is an important part of life and understanding the jobs people do helps us in getting to know about them. But when my wife was a stay-at-home mum I would get really cross if anyone dared to ask her that question. She definitely worked! She was simultaneously a logistics expert (how do you get five kids ready for school in the morning?), an industrial caterer (how do you prepare twenty-one meals a day on a tight budget?), and a hostage negotiator (how do you disentangle teddy when he has been kidnapped from one child's bed and taken without permission to another child's bed?). She was also a tutor in numeracy and literacy, a taxi driver and social secretary, and plenty more besides. But often the question – What do you do for a job? – dismissed her labours of love because they weren't paid work.

This simplistic thinking highlights the problem of dualism. In this case the assumption held by many is that if you are not working to earn money, you are not working at all. In our Christian life there are many other examples of dualistic thinking. When a "worship leader" introduces a "time of worship", they are giving the impression that there are periods of our day when we are not worshipping. When a "prayer leader" invites us to "close our eyes and turn our hearts to God", it suggests that our hearts and our eyes are somehow disconnected and can't work simultaneously.

A holistic approach to worship engages head, heart and hands and everything else for that matter; it is as active in the home or in the workplace as it is in church. J. I. Packer argued: "the health of the human soul, requires… a balanced threefold concern, for truth, for experience and for action".[187] The structure and flow of the epistles help us to see how to tie what we believe about God with how to live for God, as the epistles take us on a whole journey from the intellectual to the emotional to the practical implications of our faith.

## Intellect

The epistles are full of teaching about who God is, what he has done, and how his covenant to his people Israel is fulfilled in Jesus Christ. The

---

187 Packer, J. I., 1992, *A Passion for Holiness*, CrossWay Books, pp. 169–170.

teaching is often very condensed and intense and stretches our mind in all directions as we try to understand the enormity and complexity of the writer's logic. Look out for the flowing arguments and tight theological arguments of passages like Romans 9–11 and Galatians 3–5.

## Emotions

For many Christians this intellectual exercise is enough to fully occupy them for decades! But the epistles don't end here. Paul also fills his letters with passionate language and occasional spontaneous outbursts into song or prayer. This emotional stuff is enough to keep some Christians fully occupied for decades too, but we don't have the luxury of choosing between the two styles, picking the one that suits our personality best. Knowing God and loving God go hand in hand; it is what God has done that inspires how Paul feels. If our emotions are unaffected, then we haven't even begun to grasp the intellectual teaching, and if we ignore the intellectual teaching, then our emotional expression will be shallow and short-lived. When you are reading the epistles look out for expressions of praise or poetic descriptions of Jesus – for example, in Philippians 2, Colossians 1, Ephesians 2 and 1 Timothy 3.[188]

## Actions

Finally, the epistles move from intellect to emotions to actions. Paul argues that God's worth-ship inspires us not only to worship but also to work. Right thinking about God is evidenced in right feelings toward God and right actions for God. It is not always a linear process. Our emotions, intellect and actions are inextricably intertwined. But in

the epistles the format is one of the doctrinal teaching coming before the call to action.

If some people naturally prefer the intellectual challenge of the epistles, and others prefer their emotional challenge, it is also true that other people prefer the practical elements of the teaching. But faith is not just pure pragmatism, with a list of isolated do's and don'ts. Everything we do for God

---

188 These are sections that seem to reflect early Christian hymns the writer is either composing or quoting.

should be inspired by what we know and love about God. Look out for the ethical teaching contained in each of the epistles: for example, in Galatians 5, 1 Thessalonians 4, Colossians 3 and Ephesians 4–6.[189]

Understanding the epistles in this way will change the way we read them. It should encourage us to read each letter from start to finish to discover how the writer wants us to worship with heart, mind and soul as a result of the letter's teaching.[190] Secondly, we should read the letter with people who have other learning preferences[191] to ourselves, as they can help us to develop our areas of weakness. Cerebral learners and emotional learners and practical learners work best together to help one another discover how to live holistically in the light of the teaching.

I would like to encourage you to go the distance with the epistles. Don't get sidetracked by intellectual controversies, but allow your mind to be stretched and move on to the emotional response. Appreciate the opportunity to freely express your heart's response to God, but don't stop for too long or you may get too comfortable and forget to finish your journey – let the rubber hit the road in showing the practical consequences of what you have read.

189 These are sometimes known as the "paraenetic" sections. See Thomson, M., 1993, "Teaching/Paraenesis" in Hawthorne, G. F., Martin, R. P. & Reid, D. G., 1993, *Dictionary of Paul and His Letters*, IVP, p. 922.
190 See Longnecker, R. N., 1994, "On Reading a New Testament Letter – Devotionally, Homiletically, Academically", *Themelios*, 20.1, October 1994, pp. 4–8.
191 This interesting approach is encouraged by Ekblad, R., in 2005, *Reading the Bible with the Damned*, Westminster John Knox Press.

## TRAVEL JOURNAL: Romans 11:25 – 12:2

1. Scan through Romans 1–11 to see the big theological themes that Paul is writing about. Read Romans 11:25–32. Why is it so important that the Jewish Christians accept that God is graciously saving non-Jews? Identify the controversies without being tempted to solve them all!

2. Read Romans 11:33–36. What has inspired Paul's outburst of song? It is very reassuring for those of us who struggle to understand Paul's theology that his song expresses limited human understanding, a sense of wonder and more questions when faced with these unfathomable themes! How can you express your own emotional response to this passage to God?

3. Read Romans 12:1–2. How does Paul teach a holistic approach to worship? In what practical ways can we worship God?

4. Which is your preferred learning style – head, heart or hands? How can you redress the balance as you study the epistles?

# Day 4: **Transmission**

Ravi thought he had landed on a different planet! He had randomly posted a message on the church website asking for prayer and a week later he had arrived in England, moved into our house and joined us at our ten o'clock service. It just so happened that it was the week we had invited a Kenyan musician to lead our sung worship. With just a drum and some simple songs in Kiswahili, the building was packed and the rhythms were infecting even the oldest and most straight-laced English members of the congregation. Ravi was unfamiliar with the Christian faith and asked a lot of questions to the family sitting next to him. He listened to their story about life as Kurdish refugees and their dramatic conversion from Islam. When he got home he could not disguise how freaked out he had been. He admitted he had never been in the same room as a Muslim family before, and to see them and Asian and African families worshipping together spoke louder to him even than the volume of the singing that morning.

The church's opportunity to be a welcoming and united community in a disparate and fragmented world puts us on very similar terms with the early church. The call for the church to be a culture-crossing, class-crossing Christian community is arguably our biggest struggle and undoubtedly our strongest apologetic.[192] John Stott put it succinctly: "the church is an integral part of the gospel".[193] The church's life together is a visible expression of the reconciling power of the gospel. And so it is that we find in the epistles a challenging blueprint for unity and cooperation that reads like a car moving through the gears.

## First gear: we read as a community

Much of our Bible reading is done in an isolated and individualistic way. We have our own personal copies of the Bible, which we read when we get time by ourselves first thing in the morning or last thing at night, as though God could only speak to us one-to-one. But the epistles were written to be read in community. This is not the same as the pastor reading it out to the whole church, but the Sunday sermon may well

---

192  Missiologist Lesslie Newbigin put it this way: "I am suggesting that the only answer, the only hermeneutic of the gospel, is a congregation of men and women who believe it and live by it." Newbigin, L., 1989, *The Gospel in a Pluralist Society*, SPCK, p. 223. Reproduced with permission of The Licensor through PLSClear.

193  Stott, J., 1989, *The Bible Speaks Today: The Message of Ephesians*, IVP, p. 129. Robert Banks describes the attractiveness of "universal fraternity which captivated the minds of educated Greeks and Romans and devout Jewish leaders." See Banks, R., 1980, *Paul's Idea of Community: The early house churches in their historical setting*, Eerdmans, p. 37.

provoke us to read and discuss the letter as a family, as a small group, with friends and neighbours.

## Second gear: we read as a diverse community

There are at least six places in the epistles where the writers outline the different groups of people that would have been expected to be listening in to the reading of the letters.[194] What strikes us immediately is the huge diversity of people that were part of these early house churches. Men and women, adults and children, masters and slaves all learned together, formed into a family by the Spirit of God. This would have been unthinkable elsewhere in the ancient world. The church offered a vision of a new kind of multigenerational, multicaste, multicultural family, where differences in social class, age, gender and religious upbringing no longer mattered. As the commentator Peter O'Brien puts it: "the very existence of the church, this new multiracial community in which the Jews and Gentiles have been brought together in unity in the one body, is itself the manifestation of God's richly diverse wisdom".[195] The great advantage in studying the Bible with people from very different walks of life is that our cultural blind spots are shown up, our patience is tested, our love is proved and the truth shines out.

## Third gear: we read as a diverse and visible community

Paul writes to Titus about how the Bible should be applied differently to the diverse groups of people that were part of the fledgling church in Crete. He gives very clear instructions about the way that people in different life stages and different socio-economic situations needed to be helped to understand the implications of God's word for their context, "so that in every way they will make the teaching about God our Saviour attractive".[196] The epistles teach us to live out our faith in such a way that we ourselves become "living epistles".[197] This echoes Jesus' own teaching the day before his crucifixion: "By this all men will know that you are my disciples, if you love one another."[198] Too many churches are a negative advertisement for the Christian faith, and we need to hear the

---

194 These "household codes" are found in Colossians 3:18 – 4:1; Ephesians 5:22–33; 1 Timothy 2:1–15; Titus 2:1–8; 1 Peter 2:13–3:7. See Hawthorne, G. F., Martin, R. P. & Reid, D. G., 1993, *Dictionary of Paul and His Letters*, IVP, p. 417.
195 O'Brien, P. T., 1999, *The Letter to the Ephesians*, IVP, p. 27.
196 Titus 2:10.
197 2 Corinthians 3:2–3.
198 John 13:35.

challenge of the epistles to allow God to write the truth of them into our minds and lives, so we commend the truthfulness of the Bible and the truth of Jesus.

## Fourth gear: we read as a diverse and visible global community

The epistles were not designed for individual consumption, but were letters written to whole communities, and furthermore there was an expectation that they would be passed on to other communities. The letter to the Colossian church contains an instruction to exchange correspondence with the church in Laodicea, for example. More than that, God knew that the letters would be transmitted to thousands of other communities through the centuries. Reading the epistles brings us together with Christians throughout the world, throughout history.

Imagine reading the FIFA rules for playing football in the privacy of your home. It may make logical sense, but it won't come alive until you find some mates, some jumpers for goalposts, and a ball, and try to actually play the game, join a league, try to win a trophy and emulate the champions. Similarly, reading the epistles will only truly come alive when we relate in community with a people from a diversity of backgrounds, as part of the global church before a watching world.

### TRAVEL JOURNAL: Titus 2:1–15

1.  Paul is not promoting slavery or suggesting that the women's place must always be in the home, but is taking the cultural norms of his time to show how radical the church was. What do these verses tell us about who was expected to be present in the church community and how they were expected to relate?
2.  What is the motivation behind these codes of behaviour?
3.  How could unity and diversity blend together in your church to promote the truthfulness of the gospel?
4.  "For the grace of God that brings salvation has appeared to all men" (verse 11). How prepared are we to welcome different types of people into our church as equals?

# Day 5: **Pimp my ride**

When I was going through a very difficult time at work, someone kindly gave me a tiny wooden cross. For a while, I started taking it with me into work. Whenever I felt anxious or worried, I would put my hand in my coat pocket and let my fingers trace the surface of the cross. It gave me peace remembering what Jesus had done for me through his sacrificial death. It gave me courage knowing that no matter how bad things got, I could count on the love of God.

After a while, I realised that instead of thinking about what Jesus had done for me on the cross, I was instead thinking more about the little wooden cross in my pocket. It felt so smooth. It had brought me such comfort. It was helping me face my challenges. It was becoming a lucky charm, a talisman, a security blanket, even though it was nothing more than a factory-produced item with no mystical powers at all. Even worse, I realized that my whole view of Jesus' death was shifting. I had begun to imagine that in my perceived battle of me versus the world, God was on my side.

The Bible says very clearly that God sent his son – for the world. Jesus should not be reduced to a pocket-sized saviour or a "personal Jesus" as Depeche Mode and Johnny Cash both sang about. Jesus did not come to fight our battles and boost our egos. He called us to follow him and love the whole world.

In a world where you can have your coffee, fast food and mobile phone the way you want it, when you want it, it's no surprise that we treat Jesus the same way – a made-to-order, designer Jesus that pimps my ride best. Some like Jesus at Christmas, some like him at Easter, some focus on a strong, macho Jesus, others on the weak servant Jesus, still others relate to an angry Jesus, a listening Jesus, or a calming-the-storm Jesus.

Whichever way we like to think of Jesus, by confining him into our own preferences we develop a micro-Jesus. But the more we try to make our image of Jesus suit ourselves, the greater the chance that we are not worshipping Jesus, the true and living God, at all, but an idol that we have constructed ourselves. One vital way we can guard against this danger is to allow the whole of Scripture to help us form our picture of Jesus. The Old Testament points forward to Jesus as the Messiah and the gospels win us to the person and character of Jesus, but the epistles add another dimension, helping us to understand the implications of who

Jesus is and what he has done, and giving us an even bigger and clearer picture of what it means to follow him.

## The epistles celebrate all of Jesus' life

Yes, Jesus was a baby, born in a manger, but he grew up to be a man.[199] He died on a cross for the sins of the world,[200] but he rose from the grave victorious.[201] He appeared to over 500 people,[202] proving he was alive, but then he ascended to heaven. Yes, Jesus is in heaven now interceding[203] at the right hand of the Father, but he will come back again and judge the living and the dead.[204]

The epistles don't just focus on baby Jesus or Jesus on the cross or Jesus in heaven. Jesus is celebrated in every aspect of his life, death and resurrection. When we come across the various descriptions of Jesus in the epistles, they emphasize different aspects for a reason. Perhaps we need to learn to appreciate his humility, be moved by his compassion, celebrate his hope, trust his timing, or prepare for his return.

## Jesus is bigger than we think

The temptation to turn Jesus into the mascot that supports all my causes is strong. Jesus has been widely portrayed both as the macho Christ, and the pacifist Christ. He has too often been reduced to the poster boy for this kind of politics, that kind of parenting, this kind of church, and that kind of worship experience. The epistles challenge us to paint a bigger picture of Jesus, so we no longer fall into the trap of conscripting Christ to our agendas, but, realizing he is far too big to fit into our plans, instead we begin to fit into his.

Paul's cosmic descriptions of Jesus in Colossians 1 and Ephesians 1, for example, help us to counter our temptation to think that he exists for us, by powerfully reminding us that we exist for him. David Bosch, a South African missiologist, put it this way: "there is a tendency among evangelicals to regard Christ as the Lord only of the Church and not of the cosmos as well… concern has been for salvation from the world rather than the world's renewal".[205]

---

199 Philippians 2:1–11.
200 Romans 3:21–26.
201 1 Corinthians 15.
202 1 Corinthians 15:1–8.
203 Romans 8:28–34.
204 1 Thessalonians 4:13–17.
205 Bosch, D. J., 1980, *Witness to the World: Christian Mission in Theological Perspective*, New Foundations Theological Library, John Knox Press, p. 202. See also Walsh, B. J., Keesmaat, S. C., 2004, *Colossians Remixed: Subverting the Empire*, IVP.

## Jesus is closer than we think

When our science teacher nipped outside for a quick smoke, all hell broke loose in the chemistry lab. Kids would get up and mimic the teacher doing the register; others would scrawl obscene messages on the blackboard, while a few would inhale gas out of the taps, or ignite their hair. But when she walked back into the room, suddenly everyone was sat back in the right position looking as innocent as the school day is long, despite evidence in chalk and smoke and fumes to the contrary. Sometimes it seems like the church is stuck in schoolboy mode – not quite grasping the fact that Jesus will not be gone for long, choosing to mess around instead of taking his authority seriously, and imagining we can get away with it by looking well behaved.

The epistles not only force us to expand our horizons when it comes to who Jesus is and what he has done, they also force us to keep our eyes on the horizon for the returning Jesus. Some of the epistles are written to Christians who had given up on Jesus' return, others to Christians who expected him so imminently that they had given up working or planning for the future. Two thousand years later, most Christians fall into the first category, and so the epistles are a timely reminder that Jesus is closer than we think, and give us clear instructions as to what we can be getting on with in the meantime. This is a good counterbalance for what we will be looking at next week in our studies on Revelation.

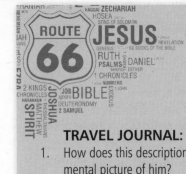

**TRAVEL JOURNAL: Colossians 1**

1. How does this description of Jesus challenge your own mental picture of him?

2. Make a list of the attributes of Jesus alluded to in this passage.

3. What are the clues here that Paul is expecting Christ's imminent return?

4. How then should we live in light of these two enormous pictures?

# Small Group Study 7
# Living purposefully with the epistles

Have you ever read somebody else's mail? Tell the story.

*Dear Frank*

*Thanks for your card – I was so surprised to hear your news. After all these years, that was one announcement I never expected. How does Betty feel about all of this – and Jan? and the kids? I would like to offer my congratulations, but at the same time express that I am a little annoyed. If it was anyone else I wouldn't have minded, but you are such a close friend that it has hit me quite hard. I guess we won't be having that Christmas drink together after all. So when is the big day? I've got a box or two in the loft that may come in handy, so pop round after work sometime. Cheers, Bob.*

Spot the clues and use your imagination to guess what is being talked about. What do you think was in the card Frank wrote to Bob? What questions are left in your mind as a result of Bob's letter?

Read the whole book of Philemon out loud as a group.

Paul does not introduce himself as an authority figure as in other letters, but on very familiar terms. What effect does this have and what themes could he be introducing by doing this?

Look through the letter and piece together any clues to see what the history is of the relationships between the people that are mentioned in the letter. Try to work out the life situation that explains the content of this letter. What has happened between Philemon and Onesimus?

What questions are left in your mind as a result of this letter?

There is a big cultural gap between the life situation of the letter to Philemon and today.

| Differences between Philemon's context and yours | Similarities between Philemon's context and yours | What are the enduring characteristics for God's people that we should learn from this letter? |
| --- | --- | --- |
| | | |
| | | |
| | | |
| | | |

Why do you think Paul concerns himself with investing time into repairing the relationship between Onesimus and Philemon?

Think of some broken relationships you know about at your workplace, in your community and in your church.

Think of three practical things you could do to model some of the peacemaking priorities you see in this letter in your own situation.

1 _____

2 _____

3 _____

Personal letters are becoming rarer in our society, but perhaps they are therefore more meaningful when they are received. Who could you write to today to encourage in their faith?

# Week 8: **Living hopefully**

*The apocalyptic literature and its application to life*

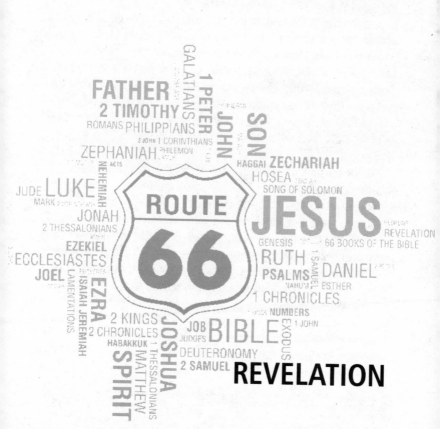

# Day 1: **Happy ending**

Hollywood loves a happy ending when it comes to relationships. Romance flourishes, the music swells, the sun sets and the happy couple ride off into the horizon smiling into each other's eyes. But planet earth gets a very different treatment in the movie industry. Aliens invade, major cities are destroyed, viruses wipe out human life, robots rise up against their makers and natural disasters sweep away entire continents. The expectation seems to be that war, technology, politics or ecology are all ultimately doomed to destroy the world, not rescue it. It is a clever trick of the trade to hold these happy endings and tragic endings in tension. The message is that as long as you have love, it doesn't matter if the whole world falls apart around you – or, as the title of REM's song puts it: "It's the end of the world as we know it… and I feel fine."[206]

The apocalyptic literature of the Bible describes the future of the world and the future of our relationships in a completely different light, showing us that there is no disconnect between our personal stories and the story of the planet. In fact, Revelation ties our daily experiences together with God's big plans for the universe, and helps us live now in the light of the end of the story. We are encouraged to persevere right to the end of this strange book, as it comes with a built-in promise that has not yet passed its expiry date: "blessed are those who hear it and take to heart what is written in it".[207]

Despite the promise of blessing and many reminders to persevere, Revelation remains to many Christians unread and unsettling. Some are understandably put off by the weirdness of the descriptions of multiheaded monsters, rivers of blood, trumpets and bowls of plagues. Some are put off by those who obsess over each detail and interpret every newspaper headline with a reference from Revelation's prophecy. Many of us find Revelation such hard work to understand that it reminds us of algebra homework or a Shakespeare literary appreciation exercise. But who would want to miss out on God's blessing? We should take God's word for it that Revelation will be worth the effort.

This week we are going to take a closer look at this apparently inaccessible book of the Bible. Revelation, like some of the chapters of the

---

206 See Kandiah, K., 2008, "Eschatology and Popular Culture" chapter in Rook, R. & Holmes, S., (eds.), *What Are We Waiting For? Christian Hope and Contemporary Culture*, Paternoster.
207 Revelation 1:3.

book of Daniel,[208] is a biblical example of a style of literature that has not survived in the West. So we will begin by looking at the conventions of the genre and how apocalyptic literature functioned in the first century, then we will look at the predictions themselves. We will learn how to interpret the images and the numbers, and finally we will try to summarize what the apocalyptic literature of the Bible teaches about our future.

## Written to reveal the hidden

The term "apocalypse" means literally the revealing or the uncovering of something that was hidden.[209] Because our attention is grabbed by the cataclysmic events that stand out in this type of literature, the term "apocalypse" has come to be understood as synonymous with catastrophe, but understanding Revelation as a book about the Revealer is more helpful. Descriptions of the heavenly realm were common in apocalyptic literature, and there were often powerful verbal images painted of angels and monsters, so the first readers and hearers of the book of Revelation would not have found the descriptions of the fearsome beasts or angelic messengers unusual.[210]

From verse 1, Jesus is shown to be the central character. Firstly, Jesus is the Revealer – he is the Lord of history and knows the answers to all the mysteries. Secondly, Jesus is the Revelation – he turns up at various points as the faithful witness,[211] as the Lamb[212] on the throne and the bright morning star.[213] Jesus is both the messenger and message – the one in heaven with God and the one on earth with us. He bridges the two realms.

## Written in the absence of prophecy

Most of the Jewish apocalyptic literature dates back to the "intertestamental period"[214] after God's prophets had finished their ministry and before Jesus was born. Apocalyptic literature typically applies the teaching of the prophets to contemporary events. Revelation adopts this style, incorporating a lot of the Old Testament imagery in

---

208 Particularly Daniel 7 – 12, the part we find difficult to teach in Sunday school.
209 See Minear, P. S., 1981, *New Testament Apocalyptic*, Abingdon.
210 Fee, G. D. & Stuart, D., 1982, *How to Read the Bible for All its Worth*, Zondervan, p. 207.
211 Revelation 1:5.
212 Revelation 5:6.
213 Revelation 22:16.
214 Mounce, R. H., 1998, *The New International Commentary on the New Testament: The Book of Revelation (revised)*, Eerdmans, p. 1.

its pages,[215] but is clearly written after Jesus' resurrection. Just as the prophets sought to call God's people back to faithful living in line with the covenant God had made with his people, so the book of Revelation calls the church to faithfulness to Jesus and to his new covenant. Soldiers in the trenches in the First World War often carried a picture of their loved ones and looking at it gave them strength when things were at their bleakest; similarly, the picture of Jesus in the book of Revelation was designed to give hope and help in the darkest times when Jesus was physically absent.

## Written in someone else's name

To help make the connection with the prophetic literature, it was not unusual for writers of apocalyptic literature to put words in the mouths of Old Testament characters to show how their words would be fulfilled. We know of various works that are attributed to Moses, Ezra and Abraham but refer to events during the period 500 BC to 165 BC.[216] The book of Revelation is written in the name of the apostle John. However, it does appear that the author of Revelation really is John, the disciple of Jesus, author of the Gospel according to John and the three New Testament epistles that bear his name. John was a persecuted Christian, writing down his vision while a prisoner on the Greek island of Patmos.

## Written with symbolism and metaphor

Apocalyptic literature is full of imagery such as thrones and seals and a bizarre variety of animals and monsters. Much of this imagery is borrowed from the Old Testament prophetic literature, such as Isaiah's vision of four-headed creatures and Ezekiel's dream of a city flowing with water. Piling metaphor on metaphor provides a visual theology that is less about literal fulfilment and more a deliberate series of tableau snapshots that point and allude to deep truths about God and his universe.

I once took my son on a work trip to the Far East, which involved a very long flight and the inevitable question, "Are we nearly there yet?" I could have answered that question by explaining that we still had another nine hours of flying until we landed, or by explaining that we

---

215 The book of Revelation "not only contains more Old Testament quotations than any other book of the New Testament, but also preserves the Old Testament literary idioms and thought patterns in a way unparalleled in the New Testament." Goldsworthy, G., 1984, *The Gospel in Revelation*, Paternoster, p. 9.
216 Bauckham, R., 1997, "Apocryphal and Pseudepigraphical Writings" in Martin, R. P. & Davids, P. H., 1997, *Dictionary of the Later New Testament and Its Developments*, IVP, p. 69.

still had another 4,000 miles to travel. But he did not really want to know those facts; his question betrayed the fact that he was very bored. So the best way to answer him was to engage him in conversation. We talked about what we would do when we got there, the places we would visit, the people we would meet, the hotel we would stay in, the food we would eat. The difficulties of a long, tiring and stressful journey were best eased by a sense of camaraderie and a common anticipation. This is how Revelation wants us to understand our journey toward the end of time. We see a lot of travelling metaphors throughout the book and we understand Jesus to be both our co-passenger and our destination. However turbulent the present, the anticipation of the happy ending for the planet and for those who love Jesus will sustain us.

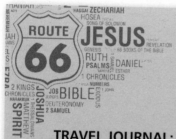

## TRAVEL JOURNAL: Revelation 1

1. What clues do we get from this chapter about what is going to be revealed throughout the book?

2. What is the promise for those of us who read Revelation and what should motivate us?

3. List seven things that John wants us to know about Jesus from this chapter. Why would this have been so poignant in a time of persecution?

4. What metaphors are used in this chapter and how do they have a visual impact, a prophetic impact and a practical impact?

# Day 2: **Predictions**

Paul has to be the most famous octopus in the world. During the 2010 World Cup Football Championship he correctly predicted the winners of the quarter-finals, the semi-finals and that crucial final between Spain and the Netherlands. Some put this amazing feat down to the fact that octopuses have multiple brains (as well as multiple hearts and legs!). Some believed in his psychic predictive powers. And some reckoned he just got lucky with a 1 in 256 chance of picking the right bowl of mussels before each match. Poor Paul died before 2010 was over – some say he didn't see it coming!

Theories abound also when it comes to the book of Revelation. Is it some sort of horoscope, a complex mathematical equation, or a piece of mysterious future fantasy fiction?

The book of Revelation was not preserved for 2,000 years just so that you and I could discover what colour to decorate the house or where to go on holiday. Contrary to many writings, the writer of the book of Revelation did not encode the events of world history in a secret formula that only the advent of super-computers has enabled us to understand. Neither did he give us a drug-induced sci-fi fantasy just for the fun of it. So how are we to understand the glimpses of the future as recorded in Revelation?

### Let the clearer parts of the Bible help us deal with the more obscure parts

Many people spend enormous amounts of time and energy trying to work out from Revelation the order of events for the last days of history, as though the book were a countdown to disaster or an early warning system for believers. But if this were right, then it would have been a useless book for all the readers over the centuries, with unintelligible prophecies and an unfulfilled promise of blessing. The structure of the metaphors and images of apocalyptic literature is best understood not as a chronological feature, but as a cyclical feature. This is also true of John's other writings and is most obvious in 1 John. Reading the letter is like ascending a spiral staircase, with new perspectives on the same landscape of God's light and God's love.[217] Similarly, Revelation does not provide us with a linear timeline for the end times. For this information,

---

217 Jackman, D., 1988, *The Bible Speaks Today: 1, 2 and 3 John*, IVP.

it is much more useful to begin with Jesus' clear teaching in Matthew 24 and 25 or Paul's teaching in 1 Thessalonians 4 and 1 Corinthians 15.

## Let the Old Testament references be our guide

The final episode of a film series or a long-running TV drama often sees key characters appearing in cameo roles, which brings a sense of conclusion and closure to the proceedings. In a play or musical, the entire cast makes a grand entrance for the final curtain call. Similarly, in the book of Revelation some of our old favourite images and metaphors from other parts of the Bible turn up to provide us with a fitting end to the canon of Scripture.

The strongest symbols in the book of Revelation are gathered from various parts of the Bible, and take us back to those moments and those significant themes. Here are some examples:

| The lamb | God's provision of a sacrifice | Genesis 22:8 | Revelation 5 |
| The lion | God's image of a mighty king | Genesis 49:9 | Revelation 5 |
| The throne | God's seat of power | Isaiah 6:1–3; Ezekiel 1:26 | Revelation 4 |
| Jerusalem | God's city | Psalm 46 | Revelation 21 |
| Babylon | The enemy of God's people and the epitome of evil power | Daniel 1 | Revelation 17 |
| The tree of life | God's promise of eternal life | Genesis 2 | Revelation 2 & 22 |

Revelation becomes a fresh way of telling the consistent story of the Bible using the same lead characters. The woman of Revelation 17 who has the name Babylon written on her forehead is a symbol for enemies of God's people, but she sits on a seven-headed beast and we are told these stand for the seven hills. It was well known in the ancient world that Rome was built on seven hills, so this metaphor not only reminds us of the old enmity between God's people and God's enemies, but shows how it has reappeared in the Roman persecution of the church.

## Note the heavenly realities that are always true

Because of our unfamiliarity with apocalyptic literature and our tendency to treat the book of Revelation like a spiritual horoscope, quirky interpretations abound and there are millions of books, websites and premium-rate phone lines which can offer us the latest theory of how events in the world today were foretold in the Bible. But Revelation was written specifically for those first-century Christians as well as all the other generations from then until now. We can't jump from the seven-headed beast referring to Rome, because it is built on seven hills, to a modern-day equivalent of, say, Chelsea FC, because it had seven wins in a row. But the theme of the struggle between God's people and God's enemies is real throughout history. Primarily Revelation describes the ongoing realities of God's reign, human and spiritual rebellion, the sufficiency of Christ's sacrifice and God's coming judgment, followed by the restoration of all things.

## Note what God is saying to others first

Apparently when medical students study pathology they can often present symptoms of whatever ailment they are studying that particular day. We too have an inbuilt tendency to consciously or unconsciously apply what we are reading to our immediate lives. With the book of Revelation this tendency could lead to stranger results than normal. We are not supposed to go looking for an immoral woman with the name of a Middle Eastern town tattooed on her head, or enact animal sacrifice in Buckingham Palace. We can resist this tendency by first noting what the Bible is saying to wider communities globally and throughout history. If, for example, we are reading about seven churches, the first things that come to mind might well be the seven churches in our own town, or the seven Christians we know best, or the seven problems facing us in our own spiritual life. But all these interpretations narrow down teaching that was intended first for the immediate hearers, and secondly as a means to help churches throughout history to learn from the successes and failures of these early churches. As Gordon Fee puts it: "God's word to us is to be found first of all in His word to them."[218]

---

218 Fee, G. D. & Stuart, D., 1982, *How to Read the Bible for All its Worth*, Zondervan, p. 215.

Revelation forces us to think beyond our normal dimensions. The church is bigger than we know – an enormous crowd of believers from every nation and language group in history. The fight between good and evil is the fiercest battle that has ever been fought. And God himself is greater than we have ever imagined. These are the certainties that are predicted in Revelation.

### TRAVEL JOURNAL: Revelation 2

1. Each of the letters to the churches contains a sentence referring back to John's vision of Jesus in Revelation 1. What is the significance of this?

2. Identify the specific and historical references.

3. Note the two Old Testament references to Balaam and manna. Check the original context to see what the key issue was in each story.

4. What is the common message between these churches and how is that significant for the global church today?

# Day 3: **Pictures**

His country was divided, there was the spectre of mass violence breaking out, and he needed to find a way to unite his people and move forward toward forgiveness and generosity. And so, with characteristic humility and genius, Nelson Mandela decided to show up at a national rugby game wearing a Springboks rugby shirt with the name "Pienaar" on his back. There were probably many others wearing the identical shirt that day, including the captain himself, but all eyes were on Mandela because of the incredible significance of his brave move toward modelling unity. The deliberate decision of the first black South African president to go to the final of white South Africa's sport, when the Springbok logo had been criticized for its links with apartheid, and when Francois Pienaar led an almost all-white team, was a controversial move. But it was the high-profile relationship between Mandela and Pienaar and their joint commitment to a unified South Africa that began to bring the country together again.[219] Sometimes a T-shirt is more than a T-shirt – in this case it was an olive branch, a sign of hope and forgiveness, and a token of grace.

As we read the book of Revelation the importance of symbols cannot be over-estimated. Here are three ways of understanding the reason why symbols are adopted in this type of literature.

### Political cartoon

The book has often been likened to a satirical cartoon where the pictures take on special significance. For example, if you see a newspaper cartoon with a bulldog stamping on a kiwi, you might surmise that England has just beaten New Zealand in some kind of sporting event. Or if you saw an eagle being eaten by a wallaby, you might surmise that America had lost to Australia. National symbols attempt to embody some aspect of our identity, and the newspaper cartoons give us a visual way of representing things to help us celebrate or commiserate, or laugh with or laugh at others. The book of Revelation uses these verbal yet visual symbols to help us understand what is going on at a cosmic level.

### Mental connection

It is very easy to find the perfume section in a department store;

---

219 *Invictus*, 2009, directed by Clint Eastwood, Warner Bros.

the overpowering aroma knocks you in the face the moment you walk through the door. But when it comes to advertising perfume on television, the ad-men have a problem. There is no technology yet invented that enables you to scratch and sniff the TV screen during the commercial break. But rather than describe the scent, or explain the chemical composition, the advertisers instead try to associate images with their product that will help you capture the ethos of the brand. So a model immaculately dressed and manicured is supposed to help us associate a level of style and panache with the perfume. In a similar way the images are used in Revelation to help describe something indescribable. Just as we do not honestly expect perfectly good looks the moment we spray on the perfume, nor do we expect the streets of the heavenly Jerusalem to be made of 24-carat gold. Nevertheless, the images are important as they fire our imagination, set the tone, and build vivid associations.

## Sentimental value

Over the years my family and I have had a very eclectic lounge. We were once given a brown tweedy sofa that literally weighed a ton. Several house moves later we had a bright-red sofa that seated all of one and a half people. We once exchanged two pre-loved white sofas for two new wipe-clean black ones (spot the family phase). And then there was the lumpy futon, the hideous orange leather suite, and the beanbags of various shapes and sizes, all of which were donated first to us, and then by us at various points in our life. To be honest, a chair is pretty much a chair as far as I am concerned, with one exception – my mum's rocking chair. Whenever I look at it, I am bombarded with memories of her sewing name badges on school shirts, putting photos in albums, drinking pots and pots of tea, reading, cross-stitching, chatting and laughing. This is one chair I will never be able to part with, however out of place it may look with the rest of the furniture.

There is a chair mentioned in Revelation too, and again the significance is not down to whether it is made of pure gold or red velvet or brown tweed; in fact the chair is not described physically. It draws focus to the person who belongs on it. God himself, the centre of the heavenly realm, the King over all the earth, sits on the throne to receive the glory and honour he is due.

## Visual sermon

The way these symbols build up provides us with an incredibly powerful visual sermon. The climax comes in Revelation 5. God sits on his throne holding a scroll that nobody is worthy to open, and John cries tears of desperation at the tragedy until God points to one who is worthy – the Lion of the tribe of Judah. But when John looks to see the Lion, he instead sees a lamb.[220] This symbolic language is placed so beautifully – the mighty lion is promised but a slain lamb is presented instead. I could not begin to attempt to capture the meekness and majesty of Jesus in words as John does so eloquently in this word picture.

Strong satirical symbolism, unusual associations of images and powerful emotionally charged descriptions combine to etch on our memories, on our imaginations and in our hearts a message of ultimate hope and salvation.

### TRAVEL JOURNAL: Revelation 5

1. Look at the following images: the scrolls, the seals, the throne, the golden bowls of incense, the Root of David, the Lion and the Lamb. What associations and emotions do they evoke?

2. Compare the images of the Lion (see the Lion of Judah in Genesis 49:8–10) and the Lamb (see Exodus 29:35–45). What other links do you see between these Old Testament passages and this chapter of Revelation?

3. What impact would this have had on the early Christians facing persecution?

4. How do these images inspire you to join the angels in worship?

---

220 It is only in the writings of John that Jesus is described as "the Lamb of God". See Mounce, R., 1998, *The New International Commentary on the New Testament: The Book of Revelation (revised)*, Eerdmans, p. 132.

# Day 4: **Number plates**

From the moment I saw her she knocked me for 6. She wasn't 1 of those dime-a-dozen girls, she was 1 in a million with her 24-carat smile and her 10-out-of-10 eyes. I think about her 24/7, and I know 100 per cent that she's the 1 for me!

If you add up all the numbers in the above description and multiply the number by itself, then hold the calculator upside down and read the numbers back as letters, you will discover the name of the love of my life. Actually, unless my wife was christened Glhbeos Geoool and never told me, I have just wasted your time! The numbers above contain no secret code, but they are more than figures; they are figures of speech. The practice of using numbers in this way was not an innovation of the Hebrews and may be found in literature of the ancient Near East before the first writing of Scripture.[221] The book of Revelation is particularly adept at using numbers this way, but when we read it we do not need to have a calculator in one hand and a calendar in the other. However, understanding some of the ancient figures of speech will get us a long way.

## Seven

In ancient times, seven was like our ten. It was seen as the number of completeness and so the Jews would have scored a perfect *Strictly Come Dancing* routine as seven out of seven. "Of the numbers that carry symbolic meaning in biblical usage, seven is the most important. It is used to signify completeness or totality."[222] The seven days of the week and the seven-year sabbatical cycle for the land are a result of that way of thinking. The Jubilee was celebrated after seven times seven years, or after forty-nine years – which was actually in the fiftieth year! In Revelation the number seven forms the basic structure of the book. There are seven letters, seven churches, seven seals, seven trumpets, seven signs and seven bowls. Jesus is speaking to the complete church and his message is that when the time on earth is completed, the future will be fully heralded and the fullness of God's wrath will be finally poured out on the earth so that we can have complete access to God's presence. When we read the number seven we sense God's fulfilment.

---

221 Ryken, L. C., Wilhoit, J., Longman, T., Duriez, C., Penney, D. & Reid, D. G., 1998, *Dictionary of Biblical Imagery*, IVP, p. 599.
222 Ryken, L. C., Wilhoit, J., Longman, T., Duriez, C., Penney, D. & Reid, D. G., 1998, *Dictionary of Biblical Imagery*, IVP, p. 774.

## Twelve

The number twelve is another significant number that is linked with the true church. There were twelve tribes of Israel and Jesus had twelve disciples. In Revelation we see twelve stars on the crown of the woman clothed with the sun, twelve gates to the heavenly Jerusalem with the names of the twelve tribes of Israel written on them, twelve crops of fruit from the tree of life, one for each of the twelve months of the year. When we see the number twelve we sense God's pleasure.

## 144,000

This is the number of people sealed and redeemed from the earth.[223] If it is a literal number, then we are most probably doomed as there have been millions of Christians through the centuries and around the world. As a figure of speech, however, the number is very interesting; 144,000 is 12 x 12 x 1,000 which seems to hint at the 12 tribes of Israel in the Old Testament and the 12 disciples of the New Testament, indicating all those who were saved in the Old Testament and all those saved since Jesus' new covenant. The number 1,000 has a symbolic significance in Revelation as another way of talking about completeness. The size of the number is huge in comparison with the twelves and sevens around, and speaks to us not of limited places in the afterlife but instead of the immensity of the crowd of redeemed.

## 666

Any numbers that are not sevens or twelves or derivatives (such as 24, 144,000) immediately set off alarm bells. When we read the descriptions of the seven-headed beasts (in Revelation 13) with ten horns (symbols of power) and ten crowns (symbol of authority), coming out of the sea (a symbol of mysterious evil), we are supposed to imagine a fearsome enemy. The size and description of God's enemy seems disproportionate compared to the image of God as a slain lamb. But there is another enemy in that chapter that is similar in appearance to the lamb and is able to perform counterfeit miraculous deeds. This fake Christ is given the number 666,[224] which has been the inspiration for many a horror movie and heavy metal song! As a figure of speech the number 666 is most likely a play on the perfect number 777 – it may seem close, but

---

223 Revelation 14.
224 Revelation 13:18.

it is certainly not the same.[225, 226] Discernment is needed to recognize the complete and genuine article of Jesus and the cheap and nasty counterfeit.

One of our favourite family games on long motorway journeys is car number plate bingo. This can take many forms. Sometimes we look for consecutive numbers and see how far we can get. Sometimes we make up stories with the letters. "NROYL", for example, could stand for "Never Reverse Over Your Laptop"! Number plates are legal requirements for identifying individual vehicles – they contain a mixture of significant numbers indicating the age of the car or the place of manufacture, and they have some random letters. Revelation contains some numbers of significance, and some random numbers. This chapter comes with a health warning – we shouldn't get carried away, as not every number has significance. Chapter and verse numbers are nothing to get excited about – they were added long after the authors had died simply as a means to help us locate passages more quickly. We are not supposed to go back and look for numbers in all the other genres of the Bible either. There is no symbolic significance in the number of loaves and fish used to feed the 5,000-plus that came to listen to Jesus, or in the 500 witnesses that saw Jesus after he died.

When my wife picked up the first copy of *Harry Potter* a few weeks after it was published, she tossed it aside in disgust after simply flicking through it from back to front in the bookshop. She claimed it was like reading a book in a foreign language, full of meaningless gibberish like "Muggles", "Hogwarts" and "Quidditch"! These days even people who never read the first book are familiar with Rowling's magical nomenclature, can recite several of her fake Latin spells, and can pick up the sequels with no explanation needed. Similarly, once we begin to understand the symbols and the figures of speech, Revelation begins to make a lot more sense, and helps us to unlock the fascinating story of the world we live in.

225 As Torrance writes: "this evil trinity apes the holy trinity 777 but always falls short". Torrance, T. F., 1959, *The Apocalypse Today*, Eerdmans, p. 86.
226 See Goldsworthy, G., 1994, *The Gospel in Revelation*, Paternoster, p. 155.

**TRAVEL JOURNAL: Revelation 15**

1. Highlight the numbers in the passage, and note how they are explained.

2. How could a church in the ancient world have taken comfort from the song that those who were victorious over the beast sang?

3. How does this song help us to have a bigger picture of God?

4. How might knowing Jesus as 777 help you to worship him better?

# Day 5: **Write the future?**

I have a love-hate relationship with time-travel movies. I love science-fiction and superhero movies. But time travel is often used as a quick and easy way to get out of a major plot dead end. Whether it's Dr Who or the Avengers, time-travel plot lines normally end up making little logical sense. But one thing that time-travel plot lines help us with is understanding that sometimes seemingly insignificant incidents can have major implications. One missed train could change a life, one wrong turn could start a war, one piece of computer code could end civilization. Time-travel movies present a future to us that is contingent on the tiniest changes. As Christians, we know the smallest things can make a difference, and yet we also know that God is the one who writes the future – that our times are in his hands.

The book of Revelation writes the future for us. But thankfully, instead of it being dependent on our ability to perform under pressure, it shows us what will happen because of the victory Jesus has already achieved. Instead of willing us to rise to the challenge, it offers us something secure and certain that will comfort and encourage us. And instead of laying the responsibility at the feet of one or two players, the book of Revelation is written to the church, for the church and about the church.

## The church under attack

The emperor Domitian was a self-obsessed monarch with the reputation of being a monster. He commissioned huge statues of himself[227] to be built throughout his empire, demanded that he be called "our lord and God", and later became a fierce persecutor of the church. All the cities of the seven churches mentioned in the book of Revelation "had the worship of the emperor in their midst".[228] When Revelation was first written the church was beginning to feel the impact of his self-importance. The powerful image of a throne with a slain lamb on it encouraged the church to believe that God was in control – not a power-mad, self-proclaimed deity, but a sovereign who himself had been killed by the imperial power of the Romans. The chorus, "This calls for patient

---

227 Beasley-Murray, G., 2000, "The book of Revelation" in Martin, R. P. & Davids, P. H., *Dictionary of the Later New Testament and its Developments*, IVP, p. 1028.
228 Beasley-Murray, G., 2000, "The book of Revelation" in Martin, R. P. & Davids, P. H., *Dictionary of the Later New Testament and its Developments*, IVP, p. 1028.

endurance and faithfulness on the part of the saints"[229] echoes through Revelation, encouraging the church to keep trusting, whatever was about to happen.

## The church unlimited

When Martin Luther King Jr delivered his famous "I have a dream" speech, he used the biblical idea of multicultural unity to paint a picture of the future:

> when all of God's children, black men and white men, Jews and Gentiles, Protestants and Catholics, will be able to join hands and sing in the words of the old Negro spiritual, "Free at last! Free at last! Thank God Almighty, we are free at last!"[230]

The speech was powerful because his vision of the future was so far removed from his experience of everyday reality, where there was no freedom and no friendship. His dream was nevertheless so compelling that the hope lifted people not only out of their despair, but also inspired people to strive for this reality, whatever the cost.

Revelation provides Christians with pictures of the future that are so vivid and powerful that God uses them firstly to develop patient endurance in us as struggles come, and secondly to put energy and passion into our step as we seek to be a foretaste of God's kingdom. For example, imagine how it would have felt to small groups of Christians meeting secretly in houses to hear of the uncountable number of believers that were gathered around the throne of God worshipping the Lamb. It would have encouraged them to keep going, and inspired them to invite others to join them.

## The church unleashed

Revelation describes Jesus as walking with the church (1:12–20, 2:1), redeeming the church (5:9–10), encouraging the church (2:8–11), and challenging the church (3:1–6). Jesus is passionately committed to his people, and one of the final pictures we are given in the book of Revelation is that God finally gets what he has been seeking throughout history: the grand reunion in which "I will be their God and they will

---

229 Revelation 1:9; 13:10; 14:12.
230 Reprinted by arrangement with The Heirs to the Estate of Martin Luther King Jr., c/o Writers House as agent for the proprietor New York, NY. Copyright © 1963 by Dr. Martin Luther King Jr. Renewed © 1991 by Coretta Scott King.

be my people" (21:7). This is what God promised to Abraham way back in Genesis 17:7 in his covenant to "be your God and the God of your descendants" and reiterated centuries later to David, promising about his son Solomon and prophesying about Jesus, "I will be their father, and they will be my children."[231]

The American highway Route 66 used to run from Chicago to California, but over the years it fell into disrepair, became truncated, was replaced by other routes and was finally decommissioned. Sadly, it doesn't really go anywhere anymore. The parts that still exist serve mainly as a trip down memory lane and have been appropriately rebranded "Historic Route 66".

Many people think the Bible is a similarly outdated collection of books, some of which make interesting reading, but only really from a historical point of view. Revelation shows us that the Bible is still in date, and that while the earth has a future, the Bible has a future too. As we read God's word we are seeing not how we would write the future, but how God has written it. We see that though there is room for our freedom and creativity in the here and now, though God has given us huge privileges and responsibilities, in the end our future is safe in his hands.

**TRAVEL JOURNAL: Revelation 22**

1. What aspects of the future are reinforced in verses 1–6?
2. What blessing is reinforced? And why is there a curse added?
3. Several times we are reminded that Jesus is coming soon. Why do we need to be reminded so often, and what impact does this have?
4. What options are presented to readers of this book? How is the church to respond to these options?

---

231  2 Samuel 7:14, 2006, Today's New International Version (TNIV), Zondervan.

# Small Group Study 8
# **Living hopefully with the apocalyptic literature**

Make a list of the things each of you are most looking forward to about the future.

Compare answers. To what extent did the church feature?

The book of Revelation clearly teaches us that our future hope and our life together as the church cannot be divided. We, as the church, must not only celebrate the hope that we have in Christ, but we must also communicate that hope to others. This dual aspect of living hopefully comes out clearly in Revelation 2 and 3, where the local church has to hear both encouraging words and challenging words.

This part of John's vision contains seven letters for seven churches. There are a number of stylistic elements, such as the use of the number 7, that lead us to think they have value for all God's churches through the ages. Read through the first two letters (Revelation 2:1–11). What similarities do you notice?

There is deliberate structure in each letter:

1. A characteristic of Christ taken from the vision of Jesus in Revelation 1.
2. A commendation of what the church is doing well.
3. A critique of what the church is neglecting or failing to be.
4. A consequence of the shortcoming.
5. A covenant promise for repentance and endurance.

Fill in the chart on the following page for the other six churches, and then imagine what Jesus would say to your church.

| Church | Christ | Chapter 1 Reference | Commendation | Critique | Consequence | Covenant |
|--------|--------|---------------------|--------------|----------|-------------|----------|
| Ephesus | He holds the seven stars and walks among the seven lampstands. | v. 12 and v. 16 | Your hard work, perseverance, hardship and discernment. | Forsaken their first love. | The lampstand will be removed. | Right to eat from the tree of life. |
| Smyrna | | | | | | |
| Pergamum | | | | | | |
| Thyatira | | | | | | |
| Sardis | | | | | | |
| Philadelphia | | | | | | |
| Laodicea | | | | | | |
| Your church | | | | | | |

Take a look at your grid. Which church do you think most closely matches the strengths and weaknesses of your church? What do you think Jesus would say about your church?

Which aspects of Christ's character do you most need reminding of?

Where would Jesus commend you?

Where might he critique you as a church?

What are the benefits and dangers of being honest about the strengths and weaknesses of your own church? How can we ensure that our honesty is constructive, not destructive?

Spend some time praying through what your response to Christ should be as a church. Spend time in prayer together:

⊕ praising Jesus for an aspect of his character revealed in Revelation 1.

⊕ celebrating what you believe Jesus enjoys about your church.

⊕ repenting of what Jesus would challenge about your church.

Revelation begins with the familiar story of struggling local churches, but ends with the fantastic description of the church as a unified, beautiful bride, shining with the glory of God, and filled with the glory and honour of the nations.[232] How does this finale to the Bible help us to live hopefully with the church?

Ask each member to talk about one way in which they have learned to navigate life with the Bible, as a result of the studies over the past eight weeks.

---

232 Revelation 21.

# The 8-week Bible reading challenge

For those people wanting to really grasp the big themes of the Bible, there is nothing that beats reading it! Here is a challenge to help you read the Bible in parallel with the eight weeks of *Route 66*.

## Week 1
*Genesis, Exodus, Joshua, Judges, 1 and 2 Samuel, 1 and 2 Kings, Ezra, Nehemiah and Esther*

*Challenge:* Read the narrative literature like you would read a novel – it is about the length of an average *Harry Potter* book. Take it with you on a long train journey or read through it in large chunks before bedtime. By the end of the week reflect on how you have come to know God as the main character, the storyteller, and the director. How does knowing a God like this shape the way you live faithfully for him?

## Week 2
*Leviticus, Numbers and Deuteronomy*

*Challenge:* Read the law literature like you would read the brochure of a house you are buying. Flick through the whole thing, then scan it more carefully, and finally hone in on the parts you find particularly pertinent. By the end of the week, reflect on God's grace to you, rescuing you from being bound to live perfectly to these standards, and consider how you could live distinctively, reflecting God's values to a watching world.

## Week 3
*Psalms*

*Challenge:* Read Psalms like you would read your favourite poetry book. Over the course of a week pick out a few that grab your attention and really meditate on them, using them to inspire your prayer and your worship. By the end of the week, consider how you could live more poetically; leading an emotionally healthy life that is marked by your honesty, vulnerability, and intimacy with God.

## Week 4

### Job, Proverbs, Ecclesiastes and Song of Solomon

*Challenge:* Read the wisdom literature like you would read a book about marriage or work–life balance, looking for practical advice for everyday help, and help on how to cope when it all goes badly wrong. How does this practical section help us to remember that every part of our daily lives can be worship to God? Consider how we can live discerningly in our body, mind and soul, making right choices with the daily decisions we face.

## Week 5

### Isaiah, Jeremiah, Lamentations, Ezekiel, Daniel, Hosea, Joel, Amos, Obadiah, Jonah, Micah, Nahum, Habakkuk, Zephaniah, Haggai, Zechariah and Malachi

*Challenge:* Read the prophetic literature like you would read a bunch of university prospectuses, imagining the university itself, and also imagining what you could become if you attended that university. We expect the context to be different, but we also expect to see problems and solutions we can relate to. There are seventeen prophetic books, and it may be helpful to work backwards, starting with the shorter prophets, to get you into gear for the longer works of Jeremiah and Isaiah. See how far you get in the week, and then reflect on how hope for the future helps us live prophetically in the here and now.

## Week 6

### Matthew, Mark, Luke and John

*Challenge:* Read the gospels like you would read four short biographies – one a day. Between gospels, reflect on the overall picture of Jesus' impact in the world. By the end of the week, reflect on how Jesus lived, what he has done for you and how you can live infectiously for him.

## Week 7

### Acts, Romans, 1 and 2 Corinthians, Galatians, Ephesians, Philippians, Colossians, 1 and 2 Thessalonians, 1 and 2 Timothy, Titus, Philemon, Hebrews, James, 1 and 2 Peter, 1, 2 and 3 John and Jude

*Challenge:* Read the epistles like you would read a bunch of letters. These books are probably the ones you are most familiar with, so choose a couple and read them from start to finish, bearing in mind that they are written to churches. By the end of the week, what themes have stuck in your mind that could be applied to the way you purposefully engage with your local church and the global church?

## Week 8
### *Revelation*

*Challenge:* Read the book of Revelation like you would read a feature article in a travel magazine at the dentist, not expecting to understand everything about a place you have never been to, but aware that one day you will go there and experience it for yourself. You concentrate hard because you know these images will help you cope in the suffering that lies ahead in the dentist's chair! There is only one short book this week, so read it slowly, allowing the images to soak in, and spotting the famous landmarks. Remember there is a promise that God will bless the readers of this book. By the end of the week reflect on God's blessing in your own life so far, and consider how you can live hopefully, whatever you will face in the future.

# Tools worth investing in

## Concordance

This book indexes all the occurrences of every word in the Bible in alphabetical order and is useful for referencing and cross-referencing. With the advent of free websites such as www.biblegateway.com you probably don't need to buy a concordance, as you can search for any term that you need online.

## Commentaries

Commentaries make the wisdom of Bible scholars available to you. They have spent time studying the original languages and the cultural contexts of each Bible book. Commentaries are useful to help you understand the key themes, structure, cultural background and difficult or controversial aspects of a book. There are a number of different types of Bible commentary and recommended examples are given for each below.

*Technical:* Word Biblical Commentary Series; Thomas Nelson New International Commentary Series (Eerdmans). These commentaries offer top biblical scholarship, engagement with the grammar of the Greek and Hebrew text and in-depth analysis of each verse of each book of the Bible. There will be in-depth articles on issues of scholarly debate.

*Intermediate:* Tyndale Commentary Series (IVP); NIV Application Commentary Series (Zondervan). These commentaries are much shorter and offer much less discussion of controversial issues. They are more than adequate for most everyday use.

*Basic:* The Bible Speaks Today (IVP); Focus on the Bible Commentaries (Focus). Whereas most commentaries offer no help in how to apply the Bible and are intended as reference books, other commentaries are designed to be readable. The Bible Speaks Today series reads more like sermons on chapters of the Bible, rather than individual comment on the meaning of specific verses. The Focus on the Bible Commentaries are also good in this respect and some of the Old Testament series by Dale Ralph Davies are particularly readable.

*General: New Bible Commentary* (IVP); *Africa Bible Commentary*
(Zondervan). If your budget is tight, then IVP's *New Bible Commentary*
is an excellent investment, giving you a single volume that contains
commentary on every book of the Bible and some excellent introductory
articles. *The Africa Bible Commentary* is a very good single-volume
commentary providing a cross-cultural perspective, as all seventy
authors are based in Africa.

## Bible dictionary
Need help working out what a "rock badger" is or what an "ephod"
looks like or where Samaria is or who David's grandfather was? A Bible
dictionary is a great help for this sort of historical, geographical and
cultural background. Baker's *Evangelical Dictionary of Biblical Theology*
is available for free online at
http://www.biblestudytools.com/dictionaries/bakers-evangelical-
dictionary/, but the single best Bible dictionary is still the *IVP New Bible
Dictionary* (3rd edition). Alternatively, a very readable resource is *The
Bible Book* by Nick Page, published by Collins.

## Bible atlas
Most of us won't need a Bible atlas, as the necessary maps are in the
back of a good study Bible, or you can Google a good map quite easily
online.

# Source material

Adeyemo, T. (ed.), 2006, *Africa Bible Commentary*, Zondervan.

Arthurs, J. D., 2007, *Preaching with Variety: How to Re-create the Dynamics of Biblical Genres*, Kregel.

Birch, Brueggemann, Frethem & Petersen, 2005, *A Theological Introduction to the Old Testament*, SPCK.

Carson, D. A. et al. (eds), 1994, *New Bible Commentary*, IVP.

Carter, Duvall & Hays, 2005, *Preaching God's Word*, Zondervan.

Duvall & Hays, 2001, *Grasping God's Word*, Zondervan.

Fee & Stuart, 2003, *How to Read the Bible for All its Worth*, Zondervan.

Goldsworthy, G., 2000, *Preaching the Whole Bible as Christian Scripture*, IVP.

Green, J. et al. (eds), 1994, *Dictionary of Jesus and the Gospels*, IVP.

Greidanus, S., 1996, *The Modern Preacher and the Ancient Text*, Eerdmans.

Kaiser, W. C., 2003, *Preaching and Teaching from the Old Testament*, Baker.

Longman III, T., 1988, *How to Read the Psalms*, IVP.

McKnight, S., 2009, *The Blue Parakeet: rethinking how you read the Bible*, Zondervan.

Stott, J., 1984, *Understanding the Bible*, revised edition, SU.

Vanhoozer, K. J., 2009, *Dictionary for Theological Interpretation of the Bible*, SPCK.

Vanhoozer, K. J., 2009, *Is There a Meaning in This Text?*, IVP.

Wright, N. T., 2005, *Scripture and the Authority of God*, SPCK.